PRAGUE
THEN & NOW

PRAGUE
THEN & NOW

J. M. LAU

THUNDER BAY
P·R·E·S·S
San Diego, California

Thunder Bay Press
An imprint of the Advantage Publishers Group
5880 Oberlin Drive, San Diego, CA 92121-4794
www.thunderbaybooks.com

Produced by Salamander Books,
an imprint of the Anova Books Company Ltd,
151 Freston Road, London W10 6TH, U.K.

Library of Congress Cataloging-in-Publication Data

Lau, J. M. (Jenni Meili)
  Prague then and now / J.M. Lau.
    p. cm.
  ISBN-13: 978-1-59223-656-5
  ISBN-10: 1-59223-656-1
  1. Prague (Czech Republic)--Pictorial works. 2. Prague (Czech
Republic)--Description and travel. 3. Prague (Czech Republic)--History.
I. Title.

DB2620.L38 2006
943.71'2--dc22
                           2006051094

1 2 3 4 5 11 10 09 08 07

Printed in China

ACKNOWLEDGMENTS

Petra Dvořáková and Todd Shaw; Kristýna Kolajová, Hana Veselá, Monika Hocková,
and staff of the National Monument Conservation Institute; Petra Krátká and staff of
the Archives of the City of Prague; Jan Jungmann and staff of City of Prague
Museum; staff of Štenc Archive Prague.

INTRODUCTION

The arresting first impression Prague makes—with her spired skyline, theatrical facades, and Castle on Hradčany hill—inevitably turns into an infatuation, as the dense urban fabric straddling the Vltava River reveals layer upon layer of remarkable history. Largely unscathed by the ravages of World War II, officially off-limits to the capitalist wrecking ball under communism, and with its historic center designated a UNESCO World Heritage Site since 1992, Prague is one of Europe's best-preserved cities, with striking examples of every major architectural style that has swept the Continent.

The dramatic juxtaposition of these varied styles gives the city its unique feel. Gothic cathedrals loom over medieval synagogues while undulating Baroque churches contrast slick modern malls. The layout of Prague holds stunning contrasts as well, with winding medieval lanes opening up onto expansive squares. Its historic center comprises five quarters: Castle District (Hradčany), Lesser Quarter (Malá Strana), Old Town (Staré Město), New Town (Nové Město), and Jewish Quarter (Josefov), with Vyšehrad to the south.

The origins of Prague are shrouded in myth, revolving around the Slavic princess Libuše, who founded the Přemyslid dynasty and, when poised on a cliff overlooking the Vltava, was struck by a vision of a "city whose splendor will touch the stars." By the tenth century, the Přemyslids had established the foundations of hilltop castles on either side of the Vltava—Vyšehrad on the right bank and Hradčany on the left—with the latter eventually becoming Prague's seat of power and its spiritual core.

Beyond the castle walls, the town was a major crossroads through which merchants, traders, missionaries, and marauders from east and west would pass. The name Prague, or Praha, derives from the Czech word práh, meaning "threshold." Its geographic setting made the area a haven for settlers, particularly Germans and members of the Jewish Diaspora. The densest settlements grew up around marketplaces located in the Lesser Quarter and the Old Town. In 1234, King Wenceslas I began encircling the latter, including the Jewish Quarter, with massive ramparts, punctuated with gate towers and surrounded by a moat, which essentially transformed the Romanesque town into a formidable Gothic one.

Over the following centuries, Prague evolved through a series of construction booms, the most dramatic occurring during the reign of Charles IV (1346–1378), when Charles Bridge and St. Vitus's Cathedral were founded. In 1348, Charles established the New Town, which was three times the size of the Old Town and, in terms of urban planning, radically progressive for its day.

Prague descended into its so-called Dark Age in the 1620s, when the ruling Hapsburgs banned all religions except Catholicism and suppressed Czech culture for the next 150 years. This period did, however, witness a Baroque explosion on the townscape, including St. Nicholas's Church and the Clementinum, both fueled by the Jesuit campaign to convert the populace.

The mid-1800s was a time of rapid industrialization, with the building of five bridges spanning the Vltava and the opening of a railway between Vienna and Prague in 1845. The catastrophic flood of 1890 spurred the development of river embankments and the elevation of street levels throughout Prague. City planners also initiated an aggressive turn-of-the-century redevelopment of the Old Town, which entailed razing the Jewish Quarter, sparing little more than its synagogues.

A resurgence in Czech culture in the mid-1800s inspired the construction of several heroic monuments in the Historicist style, including the National Theater and the National Museum. By the early 1900s, the rich democratic symbolism of Art Nouveau proved more in tune with the patriotic fervor of the times and was given full play in the main railway station and the Municipal House. Meanwhile, a clean break with tradition was made with the birth of Czech Modernism, most notably Cubism—Bohemia's unique architectural take on the style traditionally associated with painting.

The nationalist juggernaut overtook the waning Austro-Hungarian empire in 1918, when Czechoslovakia claimed its independence after the Treaty of Versailles concluded World War I. An independent state of Czechs and Slovaks was declared in Prague on October 28, 1918, and arts, literature, industry, and trade flourished. The Czech Republic rapidly became one of the ten richest nations in the world despite the worldwide economic slowdown in the 1920s and 1930s. Prosperity and freedom ended in 1938 with the Nazi occupation of Bohemia and Moravia. Jews were purged, while what remained of the ghetto was preserved as an "exotic museum of an extinct race," as it was called by the Germans. During the Prague Uprising of 1945, Nazi artillery ravaged the Old Town Hall, though thankfully the city was spared wholesale destruction.

The 1948 Communist coup d'état initiated a long period of neglect for many churches and monuments. The Communists did, however, launch several projects in the 1960s and 1970s, including the successful underground Metro and the not-so-successful six-lane highway, which cuts off the top of Wenceslas Square from the city center. After the fall of communism with the Velvet Revolution in 1989, President Václav Havel set about rehabilitating the city and backing new projects, including the Dancing House, which upon completion in 1995 marked the dawn of a dynamic new era for the cityscape.

After having survived wars, floods, fires, pogroms, plagues, Nazis, and Communists, Prague is now grappling with capitalism. Since 1989, it has attracted scores of foreign investors, a thousandfold community of expatriates, and an unceasing flow of tourists. Real-estate developers, whose numbers increased exponentially in the years surrounding the Czech Republic's 2004 admittance to the European Union, have sped development and erected more than a few postmodern follies. Fortunately, today any significant development in the historic center is kept in check, not only by height and space restrictions, but also by a growing army of historic preservationists and concerned citizens determined to keep Prague's glorious past in the present.

Around 880, Prince Bořivoj of the Přemyslid dynasty built a wooden fortress on a hill overlooking the Vltava River. Under the auspices of myriad rulers, and despite sporadic attacks and fires, it evolved over the course of a millennium into a magnificent castle complex dominating Hradčany. It included three churches, a palace, and a monastery, with each new addition reflecting the architectural styles and royal priorities of the day. In the mid-1300s it flourished as the seat of the Holy Roman Empire under Charles IV, who initiated construction on the complex's Gothic centerpiece, St. Vitus's Cathedral. After suffering neglect during the Hussite Wars and under Hapsburg rule, the complex was rejuvenated under Rudoph II, who oversaw an extensive sixteenth-century Renaissance rebuilding program. In the eighteenth century, Empress Maria Theresa enclosed the royal environs in a series of neoclassical buildings designed to lend coherence to what was by then an impressive yet jumbled architectural array.

From its commanding position overlooking the Lesser Quarter (Malá Strana), the castle still dominates Prague's skyline. It is one of the nation's most potent symbols, representing the hopes and ambitions, both thwarted and fulfilled, of the Bohemian people and their rulers, who ranged from the munificent to the tyrannical. The twentieth century saw much of the latter, with the Nazis and later the Communists commandeering the castle. After the Velvet Revolution in 1989, the castle was returned to Czech hands. Since then, its function as the seat of government has been overshadowed by its role as Prague's premier visitor attraction, with over a thousand tourists visiting the complex daily. The most significant twentieth-century renovations occurred after the fall of the Austro-Hungarian empire in 1918, when President T. G. Masaryk invited Slovenian architect Josip Plečnik to modernize the castle in the spirit of the "new democracy." Today the castle is pristinely maintained, with at least one building undergoing renovations at any given time.

Fueled by Charles IV's dream of building a spiritual core for his beloved city, construction on St. Vitus's Cathedral began in 1344 on the foundations of a rotunda church founded by "Good King" St. Wenceslas some four hundred years earlier. Head architect Matthias of Arras based his design on the stunning Gothic cathedrals of his native France. After Matthias died eight years later, twenty-three-year-old Swabian architect Peter Parler took over. His German late-Gothic designs included a pioneering net-vaulting system, forming a striking zigzag pattern on the cathedral ceiling. Duly impressed, the king asked Parler to design Charles Bridge as well, thus slowing the cathedral's progress. Construction stopped altogether during the Hussite Wars, and the destructive fire of 1541 proved another major setback. The cathedral stood unfinished until the mid-1800s, when the Union for Completion of the Cathedral of St. Vitus's was formed and construction started up again in earnest under several architects, including Josef Mocker, who designed the west facade with its soaring neo-Gothic spires.

St. Vitus's was finally completed in 1929, with its Gothic and neo-Gothic designs both constructed according to Parler's plans some five centuries apart, forming a remarkably harmonious whole. As envisioned by Charles IV (who rests in the cathedral's royal tomb), St. Vitus's is a spiritual beacon for Czechs—and also a blockbuster attraction for tourists. The top of the Baroque Great Tower offers a stunning view of the city, as well as a close-up look at Sigismund, Bohemia's largest bell, which weighs over ten tons. Located near the tower's base is the fourteenth-century Venetian glass mosaic depicting the Last Judgment, restored to its original splendor in the 1990s by the Getty Foundation. The generosity of Czech businesses is responsible for the stained-glass windows lining the nave, including one sponsored by the First Czech Mutual Insurance Company in 1929, which bears the psalm: "Who sows in tears, will harvest in joy." Echoing the cathedral's spires, Josip Plečnik's granite obelisk was erected in the third courtyard in 1928 to honor World War I heroes.

Dedicated to the fourth-century Christian martyr, St. George's Basilica, shown here in 1900, was founded within the castle's fortification walls around 920 by Prince Vratislav. When the convent for Benedictine nuns was founded next door in 973, the small church underwent the first of many enlargements and reconstructions. The basilica's massive his-and-her towers—the "female" one being more slender than its "male" counterpart in the south—were completed after the basilica was set ablaze during a castle siege by Konrád of Znojmo in 1142. Subsequent Renaissance and Baroque rebuildings greatly altered the basilica's appearance. In the seventeenth century the church was given its lavish rust-and-cream facade, courtesy of Italian Baroque architect Francesco Caratti. A century later, the complex began a gradual decline after Emperor Joseph II (1765–90) took over the convent and turned it into a military barracks.

Now shadowed by the towering Gothic mass of St. Vitus's Cathedral, St. George's Basilica appears rather modest in comparison. Behind its vivid Baroque facade, its interior is definitively archaic and somber, due largely to reconstructions in the early twentieth century that swept away many of the Renaissance and Baroque elements to reveal the basilica's original arches and ground plan. It is one of Prague's oldest examples of Romanesque architecture. During a major reconstruction carried out by Josef Cubr and Josef Pilař from 1963 to 1975, the convent was converted into an exhibition space for the National Gallery. New ventilation, lighting, and fire-prevention systems were installed, while the building's original ground plan and archaeological findings were left undisturbed and exposed for visitors to view. The convent is now part of the National Gallery and houses an extensive art collection, with items ranging from Gothic to Baroque. The acoustically superb basilica is also open to visitors and hosts regular music concerts.

Looming over the people beneath them, Ignác Platzer's Battling Titans flank Prague Castle's main portal in this 1931 photograph. The massive figures were mounted in 1768, adding a sense of monumentality to the gate that leads into the castle's outer courtyard. The inner Matthias Gate, built by architect Giovanni Maria Filippi in 1614, was one of the earliest secular Baroque structures in Prague, heralding the monumentally scaled Baroque buildings to come under the auspices of the Catholic church. The symbolic gate stood freely for 150 years before being incorporated into the neoclassical extensions built in the mid-eighteenth century. Soaring up in the background are the Gothic and Baroque spires of St. Vitus's Cathedral, located in the third courtyard. Castle Guards have been posted here since the founding of the new republic in 1918. The legionnaire's uniform, shown here, was adopted as the guards' official wear in 1929, as in its early days its ranks were composed of Czech Legionnaires who fought for the Allies in World War I.

Today, the main entrance to the castle is typically thronged with tourists who gather to snap photos of the castle guards standing at attention beneath Platzer's Titans. Every hour on the hour, there is a changing of the guards, with the noontime event entailing a bit more fanfare, including a flag ceremony and triumphant brass band. This colorful display of pomp and circumstance is largely the work of Václav Havel, who set about sprucing up the Castle Guard when he came into office in 1989. Havel asked Theodor Pištěk, the Academy Award–winning costume designer for Miloš Forman's film *Amadeus*, to create dignified uniforms worthy of the new democracy. The resultant crisp blue garb— adorned with gold braiding, epaulettes, and various historical legionnaire emblems—are a welcome change from the drab style worn under Communist rule. Havel also commissioned Czech pop star Michal Prokop to compose music to accompany the changing ceremony, the choreography of which was inspired by the precise movements of the guards at Buckingham Palace.

After defeating the Protestant Bohemians in the Battle of White Mountain in 1620, proponents of the Catholic church launched a full-scale campaign to convert the masses. One of their key weapons was the construction and renovation of churches in the Baroque style. Built in 1626 on Hradčany Hill, the Loreto complex was on the front line of their campaign and one of its most elaborate manifestations, replete with swirling stucco and a plethora of putti. At its core stands Santa Casa, a small chapel modeled after what is believed to be the house of the Virgin Mary. Legend has it that marauders threatened the house, so angels flew it from Nazareth to the Italian town of Loreto. With the help of the Catholic church, this legend spawned a copycat cult throughout Europe, with over fifty Loreto replicas constructed in Bohemia alone. Santa Casa was enclosed by cloisters over the following century and the main facade of the Loreto was added in the 1720s by Baroque master Kilián Ignác Dientzenhofer.

Long a place of pilgrimage for venerators of the Virgin Mary, the Loreto still attracts a wealth of pilgrims, though now they come more with sightseeing than spiritual purposes in mind. Thanks to historic preservationists, the Loreto is a veritable time capsule, offering a glimpse into the aesthetic indulgences of Baroque-era Bohemia. Behind the bulletproof glass of its renowned treasury lie a wealth of garnet-encrusted chalices, precious icons, and lavish monstrances. The most famous monstrance, designed by Viennese architect J. B. Fischer of Erlach, is studded with 6,222 diamonds. The collection also includes depictions of some rather esoteric saints, including St. Apolena—the saint of toothaches—and St. Starosta, the saint of unhappily married women. The Church of the Nativity houses the skeletons of St. Felicissimus and St. Marcia, each wearing a macabre wax mask. Every hour, the twenty-seven bells of the Loreto carillon, housed in its spired tower, ring out the Marian song "We Greet You a Thousand Times."

Clinging to the massive internal fortification wall of Prague Castle, the small wooden houses of Archery Lane were built in the 1500s to shelter royal servants. Rudolph II moved his royal archers into the strategically placed lane at the century's end, ensuring they were on call around the clock. Archery Lane became known as Golden Lane in the seventeenth century, when the city's goldsmiths moved in to ply their trade. By the nineteenth century, the area had degenerated into a slum and appalling hygienic standards led to the demolition of houses on the southern side of the street. Renovations in the early 1900s boosted living standards and attracted new residents to the lane. In the interwar years, it became a stomping ground for the city's artists, writers, and eccentrics, including Nobel Prize winner and poet laureate Jaroslav Seifert and Franz Kafka, who stayed at his sister Otla's house in 1917, reputedly drawing inspiration for his novel *The Castle*.

At the beginning of the twentieth century, the lane was occupied by working-class people, who would charge curious visitors the modest sum of one Czech crown to enter their peculiar little slice of Prague. In the 1950s, the lane was nationalized by the Communists, its tenants evicted, and its houses restored and painted in vivid hues hand-picked by renowned Czech puppet animator Jiří Trnka, who was known as "the Walt Disney of the East." Today, Golden Lane is a magnet for tourists. The houses serve as small exhibition spaces as well as stores that sell antique prints, Bohemian glass, and souvenirs—many bearing the image of former lane resident Franz Kafka. Golden Lane now offers an intimate respite from the grandiose large-scale architecture characterizing the rest of the castle complex. A far cry from its days as a slum, Golden Lane, with its colorful and crooked house facades, is now one of Prague's quaintest and best-preserved areas.

As the final stretch of the Royal Route leading up to Prague Castle, Nerudova Street has held an aura of prestige since medieval times. For centuries, nobles, burghers, and merchants keen on living close to the seat of power settled here, lining the street with an array of Renaissance and Baroque homes, each marked with a distinctive house sign. The House at the Three Fiddles was the site of an eighteenth-century violin workshop and tavern, and was one of Mozart's favorite watering holes. The House at the Two Suns (to the right of the lamppost) was the home of nineteenth-century Czech writer Jan Neruda, after whom the street was named. Quaint house signs proved too discreet for some of the street's aristocratic residents. The Kolowrat family adorned their palace facade with two heroic eagle sculptures, while the Morzin family embellished theirs with two larger-than-life muscle-bound moors. Both palatial residences were designed by the Baroque architect Jan Blažej Santini, who lived in a relatively understated house at the lower end of the street.

Nerudova remains one of Prague's most picturesque Old World streets. In fact, Miloš Forman used it as the photogenic eighteenth-century backdrop for the film *Amadeus*. Yet while the historic facades and charming house signs remain intact, the activities within have changed. The Morzin and Kolowrat (now Thun-Hohenstein) palaces house the Romanian and Italian embassies, respectively. Moreover, the street's characteristic quaintness tends to belie the depth of its modern history. A plaque mounted near the top of the street marks where an anticommunist student march was brutally suppressed by the police in 1948—an act that foreshadowed the oppression to come. Under communism in the 1960s, Nerudova and its myriad pubs, including one at the House at the Two Suns, became a haven for beatniks and freethinkers, including Václav Havel and the underground band the Plastic People of the Universe, both of whom were instrumental in drafting Charter 77, the human rights petition that was a vital forerunner to the Velvet Revolution.

The elaborate Wallenstein Palace and Gardens represent a colossal act of self-aggrandizement by Count Albrecht of Wallenstein, a generalissimo in the imperial army of Ferdinand II. As part of an emerging nouveau riche class who had profited from war, Wallenstein commissioned a grand residence intended to rival Prague Castle. In order to make way for his dream house, Wallenstein confiscated and demolished nearly two dozen middle-class houses in the Lesser Quarter. Under the guidance of Baroque architects Andrea Spezza, Niccolo Sebregondi, and Giovanni Pieronni, construction began in 1624 and took six years to complete. Representing one of Prague's first secular Baroque constructions, the palace encompasses geometrically landscaped gardens—replete with a stalactite grotto, an aviary, and the triple-arcaded Sala Terrena seen here. Wallenstein was only able to enjoy the comforts of his lavish home for a short time before he was assassinated for treason in 1634 at the behest of the emperor he formerly served.

The count's flamboyant commission remained in the Wallenstein family until 1945, when it was reconstructed to house government offices, and today it serves as the seat of the Czech senate. The exquisitely maintained areas open to visitors include the magnificent two-story Main Hall, where Wallenstein's megalomania is evident in the ceiling fresco by Baccio del Bianca depicting the general as Mars charging through the sky in a horse-drawn chariot. The adjoining Riding School has been converted into an exhibition hall for the National Gallery. And in the summer months, outdoor concerts are staged in the highly manicured gardens, where visitors can behold the vestiges of Wallenstein's extravagance, including the gallery of bronze statues by Adrian de Vries, depicting such mythological figures as Neptune, Apollo, and Hercules—no doubt some of the larger-than-life characters with whom Wallenstein identified.

The heart of the Lesser Quarter, Lesser Quarter Square (Malostranské Náměstí) began as a central marketplace established beneath Prague Castle in 1257. Over the centuries, the sloping square became lined with an impressive array of burgher houses and aristocratic palaces. Prague's administrative center also moved here, and is housed in the Town Hall building (in the center of this photograph), constructed between 1617 and 1622 according to Giovanni Filippi's late-Renaissance design. Perhaps to compensate for the dryness of politics, a brewery was located just next door at U Splavínů, distinguished by a Baroque fresco of the coronation of the Virgin Mary on its facade. In the 1700s, the mass construction of St. Nicholas's Church effectively divided the square in two. The lower part of the square became dominated by a statue of the merciless Austrian general Marshall Radetzky, erected in 1859 by the Hapsburg government as a rather rude reminder to many Bohemians of the Czech national uprising that the Austrian army crushed in 1848.

A busy tram stop now exists on the site where Marshall Radetzky's statue once stood. A symbol of Austrian imperialism, the statue was removed soon after the founding of the Czechoslovak Republic in 1918 and is now housed in the Prague Lapidarium in Holešovice. A statue of French historian Ernest Denis was erected in its place, a bit farther up the hill on the site of today's parking lot, but that too was removed as the political winds shifted with the Nazi invasion of 1939. Wrote Denis of Prague: "Nowhere was life so storm-tossed, so subjected to upheavals, so driven by passion, so gripped by furious and savage struggle." The Gothic spire of the otherwise-Baroque St. Thomas Church (circa 1379) still punctuates the area's silhouette as it peeks up behind the lower square's well-preserved buildings, which now consist of an array of restaurants, pubs, and souvenir stores within their connected arcades.

Commissioned by the Jesuits as part of their sweeping campaign to convert the populace, St. Nicholas's Church was erected in the natural center of the Lesser Quarter, where a small Romanesque church dedicated to St. Wenceslas stood near a thirteenth-century church dedicated to St. Nicholas. The Baroque cathedral took five decades to complete, representing the creative energies of three generations of Dientzenhofers. In the early 1700s, patriarch Kryštof built the nave, with its dynamic western facade. His son Kilián took over in the 1720s, creating the monumental dome, lined on the interior with Franz Palko's fresco of the celebration of the Holy Trinity. Kilián's son-in-law, Anselmo Lurago, added the church's elegant belfry in the 1750s. The High Baroque interior is a swirling mass of undulating surfaces embellished with cherubs and statues, many by Ignác Platzer, as well as a plethora of frescoes—including one depicting St. Cecilia, the patron saint of music, on the ceiling above the 2,500-pipe organ that Mozart played in 1787.

Today the bend in the Little Devil where the waterwheel of the Grand Priory's mill turns still comprises one of Bohemia's most picture-perfect vignettes. Known as the "Venice of Prague," the area was made even more photogenic by the restoration of the wheel and the removal of its wood enclosure. It is an amazingly peaceful little nook of the Lesser Quarter, considering the streams of tourists constantly moving overhead on Charles Bridge. In 1949, the Communists knocked down the walls surrounding the Kampa gardens, now one of the city's most romantic and expansive parks, inspired by English landscaping and with riverside promenades running along its border. The Communists also proposed filling in the Little Devil to build a road, but thankfully they were thwarted. The stream's rather murky waters don't attract washerwomen to its shores anymore, though the medieval tradition of the pottery market still thrives in the nearby square known as "Potter's Spot."

Charles IV laid the foundation stone of Charles Bridge (Karlův Most) on July 9, 1357, at 5:31 a.m.—a time comprising the palindrome 135797531, which the emperor's astrologists deemed auspicious. The bridge replaced the Romanesque Judith Bridge, built in the mid-twelfth century by King Vladislav and named after his wife, which had been destroyed by the devastating flood of 1342. Designed by Peter Parler, Charles Bridge was built using sandstone and mortar, allegedly enriched with eggs to strengthen it. Sixteen piers support its vaulted arches, and gate towers were erected on both ends so that tolls could be collected to fund its maintenance. Until 1741 it was the only bridge spanning the Vltava, and served as one of Prague's main thoroughfares. Over the centuries, the bridge witnessed much of Bohemia's tempest-swept history and suffered the ravages of perennial floods, including one of the most destructive in 1890, which caused three arches to collapse and required two years of renovations to return the bridge to its full glory.

Built in the day of the horse-drawn cart, Charles Bridge faced new challenges to its structural integrity at the start of the twentieth century. Its horse-tram route was converted into an electric tramline in 1905 and several years later it became a lane for buses. After years of vehicular wear, the bridge underwent a major renovation from 1965 to 1978, including the restabilization of its pillars and the removal of its asphalt surface. Since then, it has served as a pedestrian thoroughfare. Minor damage caused by the flood of 2002 set off alarm bells and fueled calls for a "preemptive strike" renovation. A $10.6-million, two-year reconstruction is scheduled to finish in 2007 and involves external stonework and internal pillar reconstruction, as well as the addition of insulation designed to prevent water seepage into the body of the bridge. The massive restoration is unfolding in several phases so that the bridge—one of Prague's leading tourist attractions—remains partially open to the twenty million visitors who traverse it each year.

In 1373, sixteen years after work on Charles Bridge began, Peter Parler completed the formidable Gothic tower on the Old Town bank. Over the years, the tower stood witness to Bohemia's turbulent history, with the seventeenth century proving particularly dramatic. In 1621, after the Battle of White Mountain, Catholic victors mounted the heads of a dozen Protestant nobles on the tower's facade as a deterrent against further resistance. At the end of the Thirty Years' War in 1648, marauding Swedes severely damaged the tower's western facade. Its eastern facade, however, remained intact, displaying a wealth of symbolic decoration that includes sculptural reliefs of Charles IV and St. Vitus, the bridge's patron saint. From the late seventeenth century onward, the bridge evolved into an open-air gallery, lined with Baroque sculptures portraying some of Bohemia's most beloved saints.

Today the Old Town Tower houses an exhibit chronicling the 650-year-old structure's history, and its viewing gallery offers a stunning aerial view of Charles Bridge set against the picturesque backdrop of the Lesser Quarter. The bridge is typically congested with tourists, many snapping photos of each other next to the statues of their favorite saints. In 1683, the first statue mounted on Charles Bridge portrayed St. John Nepomuk (inset), who, after having displeased Wenceslas IV over the election of an abbot, was ruthlessly and fatally thrown from the bridge in 1393. So popular is the statue of St. John of Nepomuk that innumerable tourists, who have touched it for good luck, have buffed its bronze bas-relief depicting St. John's untimely demise to a brilliant shine. Matthias Braun's eighteenth-century depiction of Jesus on the cross, having his wounds kissed by the blind Cistercian nun St. Luitgarda, is considered one of the most artistically accomplished statues on the bridge. Prince Charles was so taken by Braun's work that he pledged to fund its renovation. The bridge's real-life array of regulars includes classical and folk musicians, on-the-spot caricature portraitists, and vendors hawking reproductions of the bridge.

In 1556, the Hapsburg emperor summoned the Jesuits to Prague to further his Counter-Reformation policy. On the site of a former Dominican monastery in the Old Town, the Jesuits began constructing the Clementinum—a vast complex of religious and secular buildings designed to promote the virtues of Catholicism and directly compete with Charles University. Over the next two centuries, eminent Baroque architects Carlo Lurago, Francesco Caratti, Giovanni Domenico Orsi, and František Kaňka created a vast, fortresslike headquarters for the Jesuits, rivaled only by Prague Castle in size and formidability. Where more than thirty houses and several streets once stood, the complex comprised three masterful Baroque churches—St. Savior (shown here), St. Clement, and the Italian Chapel—as well as a university, residential areas, a library, a theater, a printing house, and the Astronomical Tower. When the Jesuit order was dissolved in 1773, the Clementinum became home to part of Charles University and the Imperial Library.

The Clementinum still operates as a vital religious and secular complex, housing the National Library and hosting daily religious services in the churches of St. Savior and St. Clement. Musical concerts are regularly held in the eighteenth-century Mirror Chapel, renowned for its stunning mirrored Baroque interior and exceptional acoustics. A bust of Mozart stands outside its door, commemorating the composer's performances here in the 1700s. Visitors can climb to the top of the Astronomical Tower, where Johannes Kepler came to stargaze, for a panoramic view of the Old Town. The majority of secular buildings now house the National Library, which contains over six million volumes. By 2010, the library will reach capacity, so plans are underway to build a new $80 million building on Letná Plain. Upon its completion, the Clementinum library will undergo extensive renovations and many of its exquisite Baroque interiors, currently relegated to the utilitarian role of book repositories, will be spruced up and opened to the public.

In medieval times, Karlova (Charles) Street formed part of the Royal Route—the traditional coronation path of Bohemian kings, stretching from Prague Castle across the Vltava to the northern border of the Old Town. In the sixteenth century, an inn called At the Golden Well was erected midway on Karlova, giving the impression that the street dead-ends there, when in fact it skirts around to the right, eventually feeding into the grand expanse of Old Town Square. The building's Baroque facade is decorated with beautiful stucco reliefs of patron saints, chosen to provide protection against pestilence and most likely designed by Jan Oldřich Mayer, who also created the St. Salvator statue on the nearby Charles Bridge. On the left stands the Church of St. Clement, built between 1711 and 1715 by the Jesuits as part of the Clementinum. On the right stood At the Blue Pike, a popular medieval tavern that was reputedly a favorite of King Wenceslas IV, perhaps used as a royal pit stop during ceremonial processions.

Today's Karlova Street offers a wider perspective because the Blue Pike was demolished along with a neighboring structure in 1903, during a massive turn-of-the-century urban regeneration program in the Old Town. A new Blue Pike building, set further back from the street (shown here on the right), is the site where traveling showman and magician Victor Ponrepo opened Prague's first cinema in 1907. Today, Reykjavík, one of the land-locked city's handful of notable seafood restaurants, occupies the building. The Golden Well now operates as a moderate-sized four-star hotel. After the Velvet Revolution in 1989, the hotel was returned to private ownership and underwent reconstruction, in which only part of the outer walls and the first-floor interiors were retained from the original structure.

After introducing the concept of the Viennese café to the Viennese themselves in 1685, Armenian merchant Deodatus Damajanus, known as the "Wandering Turk," decided to open Prague's first coffeehouse in 1714. A seasoned businessman, he chose a prestigious and highly trafficked address located on the Karlova Street section of the Royal Route. The café was housed in the Golden Serpent building, which dates back to medieval times and was reinvented in the Renaissance style with Baroque elements in the eighteenth century. In the background are several of the Clementinum's Baroque spired towers, as well as the noble facade of one of the complex's chapels, which was simply known as "the Italian." Clinging to the outer wall of the massive Jesuit Clementinum complex, the Italian was built by and for the city's devout Italian population between 1590 and 1600. Designed during a transitional period, the church is a unique blend of Renaissance and Baroque architectural elements.

Deodatus's café concept took off quickly, inspiring generations of caffeinated Bohemians to nurture a culture that thrives to this day, and one which has only recently been infiltrated by its modern equivalent. Now brightly painted—and still bearing its distinctive nineteenth-century house sign—the Golden Serpent building contains a café-restaurant of the same name. The Italian, however, is closed to the public and looks the worse for the wear. Its facade is covered with soot and the illusionary Baroque grill in its entrance portico has become a makeshift bulletin board for advertising flyers. Fortunately, the chapel is currently undergoing reconstruction, funded by Italian companies connected to Prague that recognize the project's historic cross-cultural significance. It is one of Bohemia's finest examples of Italian Baroque architecture and one of the oldest testimonies to the long-standing rapport between the two cultures.

In the late nineteenth century, the streets of Prague echoed with the clip-clop of horses and the sounds of carriage and wagon wheels running along the cobblestone streets. So heavy and loud was the horse-powered traffic at times that residents began lining the streets in front of their homes with hay to dull the noise. Located in the center of the Old Town in the shadow of the Clementinum's Astronomical Tower, the forge at Linhart Place, shown here in 1890, ran a thriving business, providing a while-you-wait horseshoe service and filling the area with the sharp sounds of metal hammering. For a long time, traveling by foot was the main form of transportation because only the wealthy could afford their own carriages. Only occasionally would the middle class splurge and hire a hackney so they could arrive at a formal ball in style. But by the late 1800s, horse-drawn coaches and trams began appearing on the city streets, providing the masses with an affordable means of getting about town.

With the introduction of electric trams and buses in the early twentieth century, business at the horseshoe forge began to falter. The forge was dismantled along with several other buildings in the vicinity during the extensive urban renewal program of the early 1900s. The massive New Town Hall, built between 1905 and 1912 by Osvald Polívka and comprised of neo-Baroque and Art Nouveau elements, now occupies the entire block. Like the Art Nouveau Municipal House, on which Polívka was working simultaneously, the facade of this building on the Clementinum side is embellished with the works of leading sculptors of the day, including Stanislav Sucharda, Ladislav Šaloun, and Josef Mařatka. Today it houses the offices of the Municipal Authorities of the City of Prague. Linhartská Street is now far narrower, open to vehicular traffic—including the occasional horse-drawn carriage—and is one of several streets in the historic center that has had its cobblestones replaced with asphalt.

When the astronomical clock was first revealed in 1410, it represented the cutting edge of medieval technology. Designed by watchmaker Mikuláš of Kadaň and astronomer Jan Šindel, it contains an elaborate astrolabe displaying the movement of the sun, moon, and zodiacal constellations, in addition to telling time in three formats: Central European, Old Bohemian (with the twenty-four-hour day starting at sunset), and Babylonian. To the uninitiated, however, the astrolabe was largely an indecipherable flourish of symbols and dials. In an attempt to make it more accessible to the masses, an hourly procession of twelve apostle figures was added in the seventeenth century, as well as a group of allegorical figures reflecting cultural stereotypes of the time—Death as a skeleton, Vanity as a figure holding a gilded mirror, Delight portrayed as a Turk, and Greed in the guise of a Jewish moneylender. In the 1850s, the clock underwent a complete renovation, and a calendarium— painted with zodiac figures by Josef Mánes—was added beneath the astrolabe.

Today the astronomical clock is the Old Town Square's main attraction, luring masses of tourists who gather at its base just before every hour, checking their digital watches to make sure they've arrived punctually. As the hour nears, Death inverts his hourglass, Delight shakes his head, Vanity glances into a mirror, Greed looks on enviously, and the twelve apostles, led by St. Peter, emerge from a window and proceed slowly around. It's a charming yet anticlimatic medieval morality lesson that inevitably leaves spectators waiting for more. The statues of the apostles are not the originals but replacements carved by Vojtěch Sucharda in 1947, after the clock tower was ravaged by German artillery fire during World War II. The attack left the clock face damaged to the point where it resembled something out of a Dalí painting. It was renovated soon thereafter, however, along with the tower and the salvageable parts of the Old Town Hall.

Elegant sgraffito depictions of mythological and biblical figures graced the exterior of the House at the Minute when it opened in 1611. In a move of aesthetic sacrilege, however, the designs were later plastered over, stripping the house of its most unique feature. Jutting out into the street, the structure served to mark the boundary between the Old Town Square and the Little Square, and it visibly broke the line of the adjoining buildings to its right. Over the centuries, in an attempt to meet its growing space needs, the city steadily and aggressively acquired the adjacent block of buildings that extended to the astronomical clock. It was only a matter of time before the House at the Minute fell under its administrative wing, and in 1896 it became the final addition to the eclectic mix of government buildings that formed the Old Town Hall complex. Prior to its seemingly inevitable municipal takeover, the House at the Minute was Franz Kafka's childhood home from 1889 to 1896.

No longer just pretty on the inside, the House at the Minute has reclaimed its youthful beauty thanks to renovations in 1911 that revealed its original sgraffito decoration. Hidden for three centuries under layers of plaster, an array of elegant Renaissance figures now winds around the building's windows, illustrating various mythological and biblical narratives. The sgraffito work, which involved scratching designs into a moist plaster surface to reveal a contrasting layer underneath, reflects the strong influence of the Italian Renaissance on the aesthetics of seventeenth-century Bohemia. A stone sculpture of a lion embedded in the corner dates back to the eighteenth century, when the building was home to the White Lion Apothecary. The ground floor is now occupied by city offices and the U Minuty restaurant, while the arcade, formerly filled with stores, is now a pedestrian passage.

The Prague Uprising in May 1945 successfully led to the city's liberation from the Nazi occupation. The toll paid, however, was a heavy one, with nearly 1,700 Czechs losing their lives in the rebellion and severe damage inflicted on the cityscape. German munitions ravaged the Old Town Hall's nineteenth-century neo-Gothic wing and decapitated its medieval clock tower. The hall was a prime target, not only because its dungeon served as a stronghold for resistance fighters, but also because the complex also housed the city archives and was a powerful symbol of the Czech nation's former autonomy. King John of Luxembourg established the town hall in 1338, with two burgher's houses providing the basis for the complex. Construction of the 215-foot clock tower started soon thereafter. Over the following centuries, a row of adjacent middle-class houses was acquired and incorporated into the southern wing. Unlike the bombed-out eastern wing, the southern wing suffered far less damage in 1945 and was reconstructed.

Clinging to the side of the clock tower, a vertical strip of neo-Gothic windows is all that remains of the eastern wing of the town hall. After the war, this slice of the facade was preserved as a memorial, while the bulk of the badly damaged wing, along with some adjoining buildings, was leveled. The result is an open urban space extending between the clock tower and St. Nicholas's Church, which is now lined with trees and a plethora of souvenir stalls. The rest of the town hall was restored and rebuilt over the years and currently hosts a tourist information center and large-scale photography exhibits. The clock tower's rooftop gallery offers stunning bird's-eye views of the city. Now seemingly detached from the rest of the buildings on the square, the lavish white stucco St. Nicholas's Church, completed in 1735 by master architect Kilián Ignác Dientzenhofer, hosts daily organ concerts in its Baroque interior.

Since 1915, the centerpiece of Old Town Square has been a massive monument to Jan Hus, the religious reformer whose radical sermons criticizing corruption in the Catholic church had him branded a heretic and burned at the stake in 1415. Hus's death appalled his supporters and eventually led to the bloody Hussite Wars (1420–34). Designed by Ladislav Šaloun, the dark bronze and granite sculpture was unveiled in 1915 on the 500th anniversary of Hus's death. The sculpture portrays the preacher surrounded by figures representing both the oppressed and the defiant, and a young mother, symbolizing national rebirth. Though considered an artistic failure at the time, the monument was nevertheless beloved for its subject matter. Refusing to bow to foreign oppressors, Hus was a natural symbol for the nationalist cause. At the time of the statue's unveiling, the Austro-Hungarian empire was in its final death throes and the Czech nation was on the verge of independence.

As a potent symbol of Czech nationalism, the Jan Hus monument has been covered in swastikas during the Nazi invasion, funereal drapings during the Communist takeover of 1968, and flowers during state holidays. Of the latter, July 6 is now officially celebrated as Jan Hus Day, while January 16 is dedicated to the day twenty-year-old Jan Palach set himself on fire in 1969 to protest the Soviet invasion. Though separated by nearly six centuries, Hus and Palach are closely associated. Palach was a student at Charles University, while Hus served as the first rector there, and both are now revered as martyrs. The engraving on the monument's granite base reads, "Milujte Se. Pravdy Každému Přejte." (Love each other. Wish the truth for everyone.)—a phrase that rang poignantly true in December 1999, when Pope John Paul II formally apologized for the "cruel" execution of Hus. The fountain that once partially encircled the monument is now filled in and lined with benches, where tourists pause to take in some of the square's innumerable layers of history.

The foundation stone for the Church of Our Lady Before Týn was laid on the northern side of Old Town Square around 1350, but due to religious turmoil, the church did not achieve its towering final form until 1511. Peter Parler managed to complete the massive main naves before construction came to a halt at the onset of the Hussite Wars in 1420. The unfinished structure nevertheless became a hotbed for church reform. From its pulpit, "heretic" Hussite preachers rallied congregations against the sins of the Roman Catholic Church. After the war, the church's soaring spires were erected and King George of Poděbrady mounted a statue of himself holding a golden chalice—the Hussite emblem—high on the central gable. In the 1600s, the Jesuits commandeered the church, rebuilt the interior in Baroque fashion, and replaced the king's statue with one of the Virgin Mary, her golden halo cast from the melted-down Hussite chalice.

Today the towering mass of the Týn church serves as a beacon for thousands of tourists each day. Thanks to zoning ordinances limiting building heights in Prague's historic zone, the church still dominates the Old Town skyline, most theatrically at night, when its multiturreted towers are illuminated with spotlights. Like a stern father figure, it watches over the square's pastel-colored Renaissance and Baroque buildings, including the Týn School directly in front of it (at left in the photo), distinguished by its Venetian-style gables, and At the White Unicorn (at right), with its late-Baroque facade. The entrance to the church is surprisingly discreet, located in a small passageway accessed through the school's vaulted arcade. Within lies a wealth of Baroque paintings and sculptural reliefs, as well as the tomb of Tycho Brahe, Rudolph II's Danish astronomer. When not undergoing perennial renovations, the church is open to sightseers and hosts both musical concerts and masses for the Roman Catholic parish.

Commemorating the Hapsburg defeat of Sweden and the resultant retreat of the Swedish army from Prague at the end of the Thirty Years' War, the Marian Column was erected in Old Town Square in 1650. Topped with a figure of the Virgin Mary, the column was steeped in Catholic symbolism and represented one of Bohemia's most significant Baroque monuments. The practice of erecting columns dedicated to the Virgin in public spaces flourished throughout European Catholic countries in the seventeenth and eighteenth centuries as a means of giving thanks to God for ending periods of tumult. Situated on the Prague Meridian, the column also served as a simple sundial, casting its midday shadow exactly across a metal strip embedded in the nearby cobblestones.

As Czech nationalism gained momentum at the end of the nineteenth century, many citizens began to view the column less as a monument commemorating their city's liberation and more as a symbol of Austrian subjugation and the overbearance of the Catholic church. In 1918, with the establishment of the First Republic, the column was toppled by a mob of nationalists, leaving the metal strip embedded in the cobblestones as the only remnant. Its inscription reads, "Here did stand and will stand again—the Marian Column." Since 1990, the Association for the Renewal of the Marian Column has campaigned to resurrect the symbolic edifice, whose remains lie in the Prague Lapidarium.

The sumptuous Goltz-Kinský Palace (shown here in 1909) was built on medieval foundations between 1755 and 1765, according to the design of two of Prague's greatest exponents of the Baroque style, Kilián Ignac Dientzenhofer and his son-in-law Anselmo Lurago. Its original owners, the Goltz family, sold it to the Kinský counts in 1767. Bertha von Suttner (née Kinská)—the first female recipient of the Nobel Peace Prize—was born here in 1843. Franz Kafka and Max Brod studied at the elite secondary school, located on the second floor, from 1893 to 1901. In 1948, in one of the country's grimmer historical moments, the first Communist president, Klement Gottwald, proclaimed Czechoslovakia's first Communist state from the building's balcony. Adjoining the palace is the House at the Stone Bell, a thirteenth-century burgher house that was given a neo-Baroque facade at the end of the nineteenth century and which bears a distinctive bell-shaped sign.

During renovations in the 1980s, the House at the Stone Bell's facade was stripped, revealing the original Gothic sandstone beneath. Window traceries, cornices, and other former details were discovered in the cellar and reapplied to the facade. Today the Gothic structure and the adjacent Goltz-Kinský Palace, with its frothy pink-and-white stucco ornamentation, constitute one of the city's most intriguing architectural juxtapositions. The House at the Stone Bell is now part of the City Gallery Prague and is used as an exhibition space. It also hosts musical concerts in its vaulted interiors, ranging from Gregorian chants to contemporary works. Likewise, the Goltz-Kinský Palace serves as an exhibition space for the National Gallery, and mounts shows of contemporary art as well as housing a permanent collection of Czech landscape paintings. The ground floor of the palace, where Franz Kafka's father, Hermann, ran a haberdashery at the turn of the twentieth century, is now occupied by the Kafka Bookshop.

Located in the shadow of Týn church's Gothic towers, Týn/Ungelt Courtyard (shown here in 1935) was established in the eleventh century as a customhouse and center for foreign traders. Here, in the enclosed cobblestone courtyard, surrounded by a perimeter of buildings and with two arched entrances on either side, expatriate traders were allowed to store, barter, buy, and sell goods freely, so long as they paid a customs duty (or "ungelt," in medieval Czech) to the king. Tariffs on imported goods collected in the square proved a significant source of income for the royal coffers, and authorities eventually took to confiscating goods from any foreign traders caught dealing illicitly outside of the designated area. In return, traders were provided with accommodation, a regular customer base, and relative security, including the impounding of any weapons upon entering the courtyard. Known also as the "Merry Court," the area was a cultural crossroads that became one of the city's most vibrant spaces and one its first expatriate playgrounds.

The courtyard still operates as a vital center of commerce and culture, thanks largely to a major renovation in the mid-1990s by the Ungelt/Spectrum Group, which entailed refurbishing the historic buildings and converting their interiors into approximately 23,000 square feet of prime retail and office space. The complex also contains the Ungelt Jazz and Blues Club, tucked away into one of its subterranean cellars, the Ebel Coffee House, and the Anagram Bookshop, one of the city's most eclectic English-friendly bookstores. Like the Old Town Square located just a few feet away, the Týn/Ungelt Courtyard comprises a remarkable array of architectural styles, yet on a more intimate scale. The Granovský House, with its elegant loggia decorated with religious and mythological scenes, is one of the best-preserved Renaissance buildings in Prague.

The narrow, gorgelike lanes of the Jewish ghetto were the result of intense overcrowding, as inhabitants, trying to exploit every square inch of space, put up haphazard structures wherever they could. The shadowy streets became a breeding ground for criminal activity and posed potentially fatal traps during ghetto fires. City planners, determined to rid Prague of the deteriorated district, launched a radical redevelopment plan in the late nineteenth century. The aggressive slum clearance widened the streets of the ghetto by removing all substandard structures. The demolishment of old buildings on Kaprova Street, shown here in 1906, began in 1907 and ended in 1910. Franz Kafka, who was born in 1883 in a tenement building at the end of Kaprova Street, wrote, "In us all it still lives— the dark corners, the secret alleys, the shuttered windows, the squalid courtyards, the rowdy pubs, the sinister inns."

Since its widening, Kaprova Street has evolved into a busy utilitarian thoroughfare lined with souvenir shops, fast-food restaurants, grocery stores, a post office, and the city council building (shown here at right). At its western end, the street is anchored by the Old Town (Staré Město) metro station. Running east toward St. Nicholas's Church, it feeds into what is now known as Franz Kafka Square, memorializing the birthplace of its namesake. A small museum dedicated to the writer is housed in the corner building, which occupies the former site of Kafka's family home. The square was named after Kafka in 2000, but only after much bureaucratic wrangling. "We walk through the broad streets of the newly built city," wrote Kafka. "But inside we still tremble in the centuries-old streets of our misery."

Staro-nová škola.

Die Altneuschule

Built in the walled-in Jewish town in 1280, the Old-New Synagogue (shown here in 1890) led to an influx of settlers in the vicinity, which would soon form the ghetto's core. According to legend, the synagogue was built of stones flown in by angels from the ruins of the Temple of Solomon in Jerusalem—on the condition that the stones be returned when the temple was restored. The synagogue was actually made of local materials and built by the same Christian masons who erected the nearby Convent of St. Agnes. The building's structure is characteristic of medieval synagogue design, with a twin-nave layout, seating along the perimeter walls, and a central bimah, or raised platform. From the latter, Rabbi Judah Loew—who, according to legend, created a golem—held daily Torah readings in the sixteenth century. Over the centuries, the synagogue witnessed the ravages of plagues, pogroms (including the bloodiest in 1389), fires, and floods, all the while persevering as the community's spiritual locus.

Today the Old-New Synagogue stands as the ghetto's oldest surviving structure and one of Europe's oldest working synagogues. Considering its turbulent history, the fact that it still stands is a miracle. City planners in charge of clearing the slum in the late 1890s decided to demolish the bulk of the ghetto, with the exception of its significant religious and administrative buildings. Even Hitler chose to leave the synagogue standing, as he wanted to preserve the ghetto as part of an "exotic museum of an extinct race," which included artifacts from liquidated Jewish communities throughout Bohemia and Moravia. Today, the synagogue holds true to its initial purpose as a spiritual center, with daily readings of the Torah. It also operates as a living museum under the auspices of the Prague Jewish community. For a fee, tourists can visit this stalwart piece of Jewish history, where Franz Kafka was bar mitzvahed in the 1890s and where the golem allegedly lurks in the rafters.

By the turn of the twentieth century, the crumbling houses in the immediate neighborhood of the Old-New Synagogue—including the Renaissance-style Wedeles house and the Baroque Moscheles house on Červená Street, shown here in 1903—were representative of the ghetto's dilapidated state: overcrowded, with appalling sanitary conditions and a high mortality rate. The area was also prone to severe flood damage; the deluge of 1845 engulfed the entire area and undermined the already questionable structural integrity of many buildings. Limited space within the ghetto also meant that open urban spaces were a luxury that couldn't be afforded, with the exception of this small expanse in the vicinity of the Old-New Synagogue, which was used as a gathering place for the community and local markets. By the late 1800s, plans were fully underway to demolish what city planners—as well as many ghetto inhabitants—considered a "suppurating ulcer on the face of the Mother of Bohemian towns."

The Slum Clearance Act was passed in 1893, permitting the demolition and large-scale overhaul of the Jewish ghetto according to plans drawn up by architect Alfred Hurtig, who called the project "Finis Ghetto." Demolition work began in 1896 and continued until 1907, clearing huge swaths of buildings and leaving only the Old Jewish Cemetery, the Jewish town hall, and six synagogues, including the Old-New, intact. Hurtig's plan also entailed laying a 79-foot-wide boulevard through the area in front of the Old-New

Synagogue, extending from the Old Town Square to the river and amputating much of Červená Street. As a flood-protection measure, the street level was elevated so that the synagogue now sits in a sunken wedge of land. Lined with an eclectic mix of Art Nouveau–inspired buildings, Pařížská is now one of Prague's most select avenues, adorned with chic stores and restaurants, a flashy casino and, rather incongruously, the Old-New Synagogue.

On May 1, 1955, Czechoslovakia's Communist regime proudly unveiled the world's largest statue of Joseph Stalin. Perched atop Letná Hill, the 51-foot-high, 17,000-ton statue portrayed Stalin leading a line of loyal workers and peasants into the ultimate socialist future. Locals, however, quickly dubbed the mammoth monument *Fronta na maso* (meat queue), derisively associating it with the long lines they endured daily in Prague's Communist-era stores. Indeed, from the start, the statue's glory days seemed numbered.

Its creator, Otakar Švec, committed suicide a day before the opening ceremony. And rumor has it that the electrician, who moonlighted as a model for the party leader's likeness, acquired the infamous nickname "Stalin" and drank himself to death three years later. The new Soviet leader, Nikita Khrushchev, denounced Stalin in 1956. Six years later, with the ideals of Stalin in shreds, the statue was destroyed and its remains stored in the plinth below.

With its swaying pendulum marking the inexorable passage of time, Czech artist Vratislav Novák's giant metronome, which now sits atop Letná Hill, is a bold twist on the many antiquated clock towers that punctuate the city's skyline. Upon its unveiling in 1991, however, it was met with mixed reviews, including criticisms for resembling a hammer and sickle. The vast space beneath the plinth, designed to house counterweights for the Stalin statue, became home to the pirate station Radio Stalin in 1990 and later the popular discotheque, Bunkr. Today it lays vacant, undermining the stability of the platform above. Proposals to redevelop the prominent site on the city's horizon include a gigantic aquarium that would allow landlocked Czechs to view over three hundred different species of fish and aquatic mammals. Another plan, envisioned by the crystal company Swarovski, involves a museum dedicated to Czech culture and history, comprising five halls based on different crystal forms, with angular edges protruding from the cliff.

In 1535, Aaron Meshullam Horowitz, a member of one of the Jewish community's most prominent families, built a synagogue on a plot of land between his family home and the hallowed site of the Old Jewish Cemetery. The structure was erected on the foundations of a former prayer house, set up in the late fifteenth century by the eponymous Rabbi Pinkas Horowitz. Built in the late-Gothic style, the synagogue originally consisted of a single aisle space with masterful reticulated vaulting supporting the ceiling. Over the centuries, the synagogue was expanded and rebuilt. In 1625, a Renaissance-style assembly hall was attached to the south of the building and, as was typical of older synagogues where only men were allowed to enter the main nave, an upper gallery for women was added. The synagogue was prone to flooding, and in 1860 the level of its main hall floor was raised five feet as a preventive measure.

During World War II, the synagogue closed down, as the Jews of Prague were systematically deported to Nazi extermination camps. Survivors of the war returned in the 1950s to create a memorial to those who never made it home, inscribing the names of 77,297 Holocaust victims from Czech lands on the synagogue walls. In 1968, the memorial had to be closed because groundwater had penetrated into the structure's foundations. The Communist-era "renovation" that followed completely whitewashed the inscribed walls.

They remained bare until 1989, when Czech president Václav Havel commissioned the rewriting of the names in a painstaking process that took several years. In 1997, U.S. Secretary of State Madeleine Albright, who was raised Catholic, came here to see proof that her paternal grandparents were in fact of Jewish ancestry and killed in the Holocaust. The Pinkas Synagogue also houses an exhibit of drawings by children interned at Terezín, which operated as a transit point to the Nazi extermination camps.

In an interesting twist of chronological symmetry, the last synagogue in the Jewish ghetto was built on the site of its first house of prayer. The latter, known as the Old School, came into existence nearly a millennium ago. An island amid Christian territory, it was the spiritual center for Prague's Jews, particularly the Orthodox, until the Old-New Synagogue usurped its position in the late thirteenth century. In 1868, the Old School was demolished and replaced with the Spanish Synagogue, seen at left in this 1912 photograph, which was built to accommodate the needs of a growing community of Reform Jews. Designed in the Moorish style by Ignác Ullmann, the building is a square plan centered on a splendid domed space and supported by a cast-iron frame. The stunning interior work, designed by architects Antonín Baum and Bedřich Münzberger, is a low arabesque of stylized Moorish motifs in brilliant reds, greens, and blues, with gold trim.

Inspired by the Alhambra mosque in Granada, the Spanish Synagogue is one of the most exotic structures in the Jewish town, which is now known as Josefov. The once-freestanding synagogue, however, is now hemmed in on three sides by a new annex, leaving only its western facade exposed to the street. Designed by Karel Pecánek in the functionalist style, the new annex was wrapped around the Vězeňská Street side of the building in 1935. During World War II, the annex served as a Jewish hospital. Today it houses a café and offices, and serves as a rather staid vestibule for the elaborately decorated synagogue. The synagogue is part of the Jewish museum complex and contains an exhibition dedicated to the history of the Jews in Bohemia and Moravia. It is also open for musical concerts featuring the works of such composers as Antonín Dvořák, Gustav Mahler, Joseph Ravel, and František Škroup, who wrote the Czech national anthem and served as the synagogue's organist in the mid-nineteenth century.

For centuries, the peripheral band of land on the Vltava's right bank, lying just outside the Old Town's fortification walls, was neglected and even used as a municipal garbage dump. It wasn't until the mid-1800s, when a series of events in the vicinity—including the dismantling of the city walls and the construction of an embankment and a footbridge across the river—led to the area's development. Wishing to express their "provincial patriotic feelings," the Czech Savings Bank decided in 1872 to build a cultural center here.

Named after the Austrian crown prince, the Rudolfinum—also known as the House of Artists—was constructed between 1876 and 1884. Shown here around 1895, the handsome neo-Renaissance building was decorated with sculptures of sphinxes, lions, and leading composers, and designed by Josef Zítek and Josef Schulz, the professor-student duo who were concurrently working on the National Theater. Housing a large-scale concert hall and art gallery, the Rudolfinum became one of the city's main cultural venues.

With the founding of the New Republic in 1918, the Rudolfinum became the seat of parliament. The Nazis later turned it back into a concert hall, dubbed the "German House of Arts," and ordered the removal of the statue of Jewish composer Felix Mendelssohn-Bartholdy from the facade. However, the workmen accidentally removed the sculpture of Richard Wagner, Hitler's favorite composer, instead. In 1946, after the country's liberation, the Rudolfinum became home to the Czech Philharmonic Orchestra and the first Prague Spring Music Festival, held annually ever since. Flood-prevention measures led to leveling the ground around the building. The square out front, known as Red Army Square under Communist rule, is now known as Jan Palach Square in memory of the Czech student who immolated himself in 1969 in protest of the Soviet invasion. Thanks to a major modernization in the early 1990s, the Rudolfinum has reclaimed its original purposes, operating as Prague's premier concert hall and one of its leading contemporary art galleries.

In 1911, wholesale merchant František Josef Herbst commissioned Josef Gočár to design a department store on Celetná Street. The result was the House at the Black Madonna, one of Prague's first and finest Cubist structures, representing an architectural style unique to Czech culture. Gočár, a protégé of the godfather of Czech Modernism, Jan Kotěra, was only thirty-one at the time and had no major projects under his belt, except for the Wenke department store in Jaroměř, which had apparently impressed his patron. Gočár utilized a reinforced concrete frame, which enabled him to line the building with large, deep-set bay windows, emphasizing the structure's three-dimensional quality. Meanwhile, the two-tiered mansard roof with dormer windows was designed to harmonize with the nearby Baroque and Renaissance buildings. Gočár's original plan had actually been rejected by municipal authorities for having too many protrusions and acute angles. He responded with a toned-down version—radical yet unobtrusive, and in perfect sync with its historic surroundings.

As Cubism fell out of favor, the original beauty of Gočár's building began to fade. In the 1940s, functionalist alterations included replacing the dark-wood framework of the street-level display windows with steel frames and dividing the large interior spaces into small offices. Fortunately, a major renovation by Karel Prager in 1994 restored Gočár's original design and revived the building that had been sorely neglected under communism. In particular, the eponymous Black Madonna sculpture mounted on the facade was cleaned and regilded, and now stands as a brilliant Baroque remnant of the seventeenth-century house that originally occupied the site. The ground floor houses a bookshop and a Cubist design store, while the upper floors are occupied by a permanent exhibition on Czech Cubism. In 2005, the Grand Café Orient reopened on the first floor. After an eighty-year hiatus, it has been restored to its former glory—replete with elegant Cubist lighting fixtures, metal fittings, and furnishings, all based on Gočár's original designs.

In an attempt to boost Bohemia's cultural profile, the eighteenth-century aristocrat Count Nostic-Rieneck commissioned a new theater in Prague. Opened in 1783 on the site of a medieval fruit market, the Nostic Theater was conceived as a Baroque design, but was reworked by Antonín Haffenecker in the neoclassical style, including a facade flanked by Corinthian columns. Above the door the inscription "Patriae et Musis" (Homeland and Muses) reflected the nationalistic pride associated with the new cultural venue. Over the centuries, however, control of the theater would ricochet between Czechs and Germans, each promoting performances in their native tongues. In 1786, Mozart conducted *The Marriage of Figaro* here, and returned from his native Austria the following year with the world premiere of *Don Giovanni*. Numerous Czech works also debuted here, such as Josef Kajetán Tyl's *The Bagpiper* (1834), which included František Škroup's song "Where Is My Home" that eventually became the Czech national anthem.

When Czech film director Miloš Forman filmed the Academy Award–winning film *Amadeus*, this theater, with its lavish jewel-box interior, was the natural choice for a setting, requiring minimal alterations besides the addition of chandeliers. Now known as the Estates Theater (Stavovské Divadlo), and unofficially as "Mozart's Theater," it is one of the best-preserved and most stunning historic theaters in Europe. The last extensive reconstruction, from 1983 to 1990, modernized the theater's technical elements, including updating the actors' facilities and installing equipment for shifting scenery. Not surprisingly, the theater stages Mozart's *Don Giovanni* and other traditional works on a regular basis. It has also made a habit of premiering significant modern Czech works, including former president Václav Havel's play *The Garden Party* (1963), a brilliant satire on the absurdity of totalitarian bureaucracy, as well as Martin Smolka's *Nagano* (2004), an opera commemorating the Czech men's hockey team's gold medal at the 1998 Olympics.

Founded by Emperor Charles IV in 1348, Charles University (also known by its Latin-derived name, Carolinum) was the first university in Central Europe, modeled after the great institutions of Paris and Bologna. In the beginning, however, it lacked a permanent home. Lectures took place in various locales, including the homes of professors, while ceremonies were often held at St. Vitus's Cathedral at Hradčany. In 1383, King Wenceslas IV obtained the Gothic house of Prague burgher Jan Rotlev, located next to the fruit market in the Old Town, and had it adapted to suit the needs of the university. A chapel was constructed, as well as an amphitheater for lectures, including some by Jan Hus, the outspoken religious reformer who served as one of the university's first chancellors. Hus's rousing lectures against the dogma of the Roman Catholic Church led to his being burned at the stake for heresy in 1415, and the Carolinum subsequently became one of the Hussite rebellion's key strongholds.

Charles University suffered radical repression under the Nazis and Communists, and many of its student leaders and teachers were purged. It wasn't until the Velvet Revolution that the institution regained its freedom and began rebuilding. Today it is a thriving institution, operating out of numerous buildings scattered throughout Prague, but the Carolinum complex remains its historical core. The vaulted ground floor of Rotlev's house now hosts art exhibitions, while the oriel (shown here), decorated with traceries and gargoyles, stands as a glorious remnant of the university's Gothic origins. From 1946 to 1965, Jaroslav Fragner oversaw the construction of a modern administrative building adjoining the historic complex. A long-standing symbol of intellectual freedom and student rebellion, the Carolinum was the site of the 1969 funeral ceremonies of student Jan Palach, who immolated himself in protest of the Soviet invasion. Mourners crowded into the courtyard where a statue of Jan Hus—who, like Palach, martyred himself for his ideals—stands to this day.

The Rotunda of the Holy Cross was built in the late 1100s on Konviktská Street, which was then one of the Old Town's vital arteries, linking Vyšehrad to the main river crossing. The rotunda—measuring 20 feet in diameter, with a conical roof and lantern window—is one of Bohemia's finest examples of Romanesque architecture. Romanesque buildings started appearing in Prague in the eleventh century, marking a distinct shift from timber constructions to more permanent ones made of rough-hewn stone blocks, often formed of clay quarried from nearby White Mountain. In the 1860s, after plans to replace the rotunda with a tenement block were met with vehement protest, the rotunda was purchased by the City of Prague and renovated. Under the supervision of architect Ignác Ullmann, restoration work included constructing a new altar, adding a cast-iron railing around the exterior, and preserving fragments of the fourteenth-century wall painting found in the church nave.

Today the Rotunda of the Holy Cross sits discreetly on its corner lot, hemmed in by larger buildings in the vicinity. Konviktská Street is no longer a busy trade route, but rather it is one of the Old Town's quaint cobblestone backstreets, removed from the beaten tourist track. The rotunda is one of three surviving Romanesque rotundas in Prague; the other two are the eleventh-century Rotunda of St. Martin at Vyšehrad and the Rotunda of St. Longinus on Na Rybníčku Street in the New Town. Representing the earliest remaining religious buildings in the country, all three are small—16–20 feet in diameter—with an adjoining apse, and topped with conical roofs with lanterns. The Rotunda of the Holy Cross is now run by the Old Catholic Church, which holds regular services that are worth attending, if only for a look at the preserved fragments of the fourteenth-century frescoes depicting the coronation of the Virgin Mary that embellish the church's interior.

When Charles IV founded the New Town in 1348, his farsighted urban-planning scheme involved the creation of open market areas and grand boulevards, in stark contrast to the Old Town's narrow, winding medieval lanes. The grandest boulevard, Wenceslas Square (Václavské Náměstí), measuring 2,460 feet long and 197 feet wide, linked the fortification walls of the Old Town and New Town, bisecting the latter into two areas—one situated around the Hay Market and the other around the Cattle Market. Wenceslas Square was originally known as the Horse Market, as horses were traded here regularly—along with fabrics, weapons, and agricultural products. At the upper end of the square stood Horse Gate, one of the main portals along the New Town's fortification wall. It was torn down in 1876 and replaced by the monumental National Museum in 1890. The square's rural character further gave way in the late nineteenth century, with the installation of electric street lamps and an electric tramline, as seen in this 1900 photograph.

Key moments of Prague's modern history have unfolded along Wenceslas Square—with Czech nationalists, Nazi troops, Soviet tanks, Communist apparatchiks, student protesters, and Velvet Revolutionaries traversing its length in symbolic displays of ascendance over the years. Today the square is the marching ground of strolling tourists, with locals deftly maneuvering around them as they go about their day. A thriving commercial boulevard, the square combines the extreme aspects of Western consumerism: from high-

fashion boutiques to souvenir stores, from five-star hotels to modest hostels. Moreover, the city's history is beautifully reflected in the square's vast array of buildings, including the Art Nouveau Hotel Europa, built around 1905, and the streamlined 1920s Baťa shoe store, an exquisite example of functionalist architecture. Once a major tram thoroughfare, the square saw its last tram in 1980 when construction was completed on the new Metro system that runs beneath its length.

Though not always thrilled with their Hapsburg rulers, Bohemians had no real qualms about embracing the concept of the Viennese café. From its birthplace in the Austrian capital in the mid-1600s, the institution spread throughout the Austro-Hungarian empire, winning devotees from Krakow to Budapest. By the late 1800s, Viennese-style coffeehouses were an integral part of daily life in Prague. The busy intersection of Wenceslas Square and Na Příkopě Street alone was home to several competing cafés—including Café Edison, Café Viennese, and Café Kaiser. All three were located in upper-floor spaces above street-level dry-goods stores, offering patrons wide views of the surrounding New Town streetscape. With the price of admission being a cup of coffee, these cafés served as living rooms and social clubs, where one could mingle with every sector of society, engage in heated debates, read newspapers, play chess, eat strudel, and generally while away the hours.

The site of the former Café Kaiser was cleared in the 1970s during the construction of the Můstek metro station directly beneath it. As a result, the neighboring Lindt department store—built in 1926 by leading functionalist architect Ludvík Kysela—served as a striking corner building for several decades. Today the Lindt building, seen here on the far right, sits in the shadow of the large-scale glass-and-steel Palác Euro, which was erected on the corner lot in 2002 by the developer Metrostav. After a storm of controversy that resulted in a reduction of the structure's planned volume and height, Palác Euro was given the go-ahead. Designed by the studio DaM, the multipurpose structure contains offices and retail businesses, including the French fashion retailer Promod, on its spacious ground floor. Its curved glass surface streamlines into the neighboring modern Lindt and Baťa buildings while coolly reflecting the ornate historic facades of nearby structures.

As the Christmas carol indicates, Good King Wenceslas, the tenth-century king of Bohemia, was a virtuous and pious leader. Brutally murdered by his pagan brother and successor to the throne, Wenceslas became one of Bohemia's most beloved martyrs and patron saints, as well as a potent symbol for the emerging Czech national identity in the late 1800s. Not surprisingly, the majestic equestrian statue of Wenceslas, mounted in 1913 at the upper end of Wenceslas Square, acted as a powerful magnet for thousands of Czechs who spilled into the streets on October 18, 1918, in celebration of their hard-won independence and the end of Hapsburg domination. Designed by Josef Václav Myslbek, the statue portrays an armor-clad Wenceslas flanked by statues of other Czech patron saints, including Agnes, Procopius, Adalbert, and Wenceslas's grandmother Ludmila. An inscription on the base reads: "Saint Wenceslas, duke of the Czech land, prince of ours, do not let perish us nor our descendants."

When Czechs say "meet at the horse," they are referring to the equestrian statue of St. Wenceslas, which sits atop the city's heavily trafficked Muzeum metro station and is a natural gathering place. In the twentieth century, the Good King has found himself at the center of the country's colorful history on more than a few occasions—drawing tourists, protesters, politicians, soldiers, street performers, and prostitutes into his orbit over the years. The Nazis and, later, the Communists staged ceremonial demonstrations of allegiance around this potent national symbol. And when Warsaw Pact tanks rolled down Wenceslas Square in 1968, the monument was draped with a Czech flag and surrounded by masses of protesters. In the following year, Charles University student Jan Palach would immolate himself here in further protest of the Soviet invasion. The Good King, however, would witness a new dawn in 1989, when 250,000 people gathered round him to "ring out" communism with a collective jangling of keys.

On the initiative of Count Kašpar Maria Šternberk and other patriotic Czech nobles, a museum dedicated to Bohemian natural science and history was founded in 1818. In the beginning, the count's private collection formed the basis of the museum, which was housed in the Šternberk Palace and later in the Nostic Palace on Na Příkopě Street. The burgeoning of both the museum collection and nationalist fervor soon fueled the search for a permanent home, and in 1885 the foundation stone for the museum was laid near the site of the former Horse Gate, prominently located at the top of Wenceslas Square. Josef Schulz's neo-Renaissance design centered on a lofty pantheon, crowned with a vaulted dome and cupola. Leading artists of the day embellished the magnificent structure with a wealth of statues, paintings, and reliefs celebrating significant figures and events in Czech history. Representing a major milestone in the Czech national revival, the National Museum (Národní Muzeum) opened in 1891 amid much patriotic fanfare.

Crowning the top of Wenceslas Square, the National Museum now shelters an extensive collection that includes 10,000 rock specimens, a whale skeleton, and a woolly mammoth. It also hosts social events in the lavish pantheon, as well as chamber and choral concerts in its acoustically superb inner hall. Unfortunately, the original grandeur of its entrance was obscured by the construction of a divided highway in the 1970s, cutting the building off from the square and leaving it stranded on an island of its own. Since its opening, the museum has not undergone a major renovation despite having endured two military attacks—one in 1945, when several unexploded bombs fell on it, and another in 1968, when its facade was peppered with Soviet bullets. Moreover, the construction of the metro beneath it has affected its structural integrity. Once funds are secured, the museum administration plans to undertake a full-scale restoration, including installing air conditioning and new electrical wiring, as well as sprucing up the museum's timeworn displays.

A fortress of finance flanked by two cultural palaces, Prague's Stock Exchange building was erected in 1938 between the relatively flamboyant neo-Renaissance structures of the National Museum and the State Opera. Designed by Jaroslav Rössler, the no-nonsense, granite-clad structure featured minimal decorative elements, other than the bronze male statues representing Industry and Trade placed at its entrance. Fittingly, the building was located across the street from the former Horse Market—the city's first commodity exchange, where corn, sugar, and other agricultural products were traded before the construction of the National Museum. Prague's stock market was booming when Rössler's building was constructed. The onset of World War II, however, brought all trade to an abrupt halt. In the postwar Communist period, the stock exchange, part of a shunned capitalist system, was shut down and the building was given a new role as home to the Federal Assembly.

By the 1960s, the bloated ranks of Communist Party politicians and bureaucrats had outgrown the old exchange building, and tenders were taken for extension proposals. Czech architect Karel Prager emerged the winner, and his design was begun in 1967 and finished five years later. A symbol of Communist totalitarianism, Prager's design was essentially a hulking mass of glass-and-steel that encapsulated the older building. The steel superstructure was set atop pillars built using a system of Vierendeel trusses, the same method used in the construction of the World Trade Center Twin Towers in New York. After the fall of communism, Václav Havel offered the building (for one Czech crown a year) to Radio Free Europe (now Radio Free Europe/Radio Liberty), whose broadcasts had been a lifeline for many caught behind the Iron Curtain. RFE/RL—which since 9/11 has been a target of numerous terrorist threats—is due to move its headquarters to a new location in Prague, far removed from the city center, where it might pose a risk to the general public.

With an impressive seating capacity of 3,000, Prague's New Town Theater (inset) was built on the edge of the New Town in 1858. In the winter, large crowds would huddle within its spacious interior to watch opera, plays, and circus acts, or to attend lavish winter balls. The large wooden theater-in-the-round, lined with uninsulated glass windows, however, was a fire hazard and was impossible to heat in the winter. The need for a more sophisticated building dedicated to Czech theater arts was apparent, and on May 16, 1868, the National Theater foundation stone was laid on a riverside site. That very same day, Czech composer Bedřich Smetana's opera *Dalibor* premiered back at the New Town Theater and was panned by several Czech critics, who found the libretto too "Wagnerian." As the National Theater grew into a thriving bastion of Czech nationalism and culture, the New Town Theater grew increasingly obsolete, and in 1885 it was torn down. Seen here is the New German Theater, which opened on the site of the New Town Theater in 1888.

In a do-or-die attempt to assert Teutonic culture in the face of Czech nationalism, the New German Theater opened in 1888 with Wagner's opera *The Mastersingers of Nürnberg*. Built to rival the National Theater, it was designed by architects Ferdinand Fellner and Hermann Helmer, the Viennese duo who constructed over fifty theaters throughout the Austro-Hungarian empire. The grand portal of the neo-Renaissance theater comprises a columned loggia topped with a decorative pediment and statues of artistic muses, while the neo-Rococo interior is a swirling mass of stucco and putti. As the political winds shifted, the theater was renamed the May 5th Theater after the uprising against occupying Nazi troops. In 1948, after merging with the National Theater under communism, it was renamed the Smetana Theater and a huge red star was mounted atop the stage curtain. Now known as the State Opera (Státní Opera), the theater has been thoroughly renovated and produces a remarkably wide musical repertoire that belies its strictly German origins.

The last quarter of the nineteenth century saw construction boom on the main boulevard along the New Town's southeastern border. Running perpendicular to Wenceslas Square, the main artery welcomed the arrival of the National Museum (1890), the New German Theater (1888), and Prague's original main train station (1871), shown here in 1901. Designed by architects Ignác Ullmann and his brother-in-law, Antonín Barvitius, the neo-Renaissance station was built to meet the needs of the increasingly industrialized nation and to ease the flow of traffic on the nearby Masaryk Station, where the very first train had arrived in the capital in 1845. Taking its aesthetic cues from the Masaryk Station, the new station featured a main central hall flanked by two square towers and arcaded hall extensions. By the end of the nineteenth century, the city had outgrown the main station, and in 1899 an architectural competition was held to find a replacement.

A synthesis of turn-of-the-century structural engineering and Art Nouveau aesthetics, the Main Train Station (Hlavní Nádraží) opened in 1909. Designed by Josef Fanta, the building is situated around a grand half-domed ticket hall, with administrative halls on either side. In the rear, trains pull into tracks beneath a glass-and-steel canopy. Out front, facing the New Town, the station's triumphal arched portal, flanked by two towers topped with glass globes, originally served as the city's symbolic gateway. Today, this entrance is rendered obsolete by the infamous six-lane highway built across it in the 1970s. The station is now entered through an underpass leading to the drab, Communist-built lower levels. A low-ceilinged, flourescently lit underground extension houses the main ticket hall, as well as an expanse of food stalls. Although the original station has been left to decay, the Fanta Café, operating quietly out of the former ticket hall, offers a glimpse into grander times.

The large triangular expanse known as the Hay Market (Senovážné Náměstí) forms the easternmost node of the so-called Golden Cross, which Charles IV used as a schematic basis for the layout of the New Town in 1348. The upper and lower ends of Wenceslas Square and the Cattle Market in the west complete the cross formation. The Hay Market's focal point was the weigh bridge, where wagons laden with hay, straw, or grain drove onto the platform scale built flush with the roadway. In the background is Henry Tower (Jindřišská věž), which was built on the site of an earlier wooden tower in 1599, under the auspices of the Church of St. Henry across the street. Coupled with the fifteenth-century New Town Tower located at the Cattle Market, Henry Tower lent a certain visual symmetry to the skyline of the Golden Cross. In the 1870s, the tower was given a neo-Gothic facelift, courtesy of Josef Mocker.

From without, Henry Tower looks as medieval as ever. Its antiquated stonemasonry exterior, however, is just a shell, as its interior has been gutted and filled in with a modern ferro-cement self-supporting tower. This "tower within a tower," designed by Jiří Vrzal in 2002, now houses a café, stores, and an exhibition fittingly dedicated to Prague's "one hundred spires." Original elements on the upper floors were retained, including a wooden truss from 1879 on the tenth floor. And on the eighth floor, one can dine beneath the 1,500-pound sixteenth-century "Maria" bell at Restaurant Zvonice. Where the weigh bridge once was now stands a massive neo-Renaissance office building constructed in 1916 for the Sugar Industry Insurance Company by architect Josef Zasche. In the 1990s it housed IPB, the nation's third-largest banking institution, until a scandal forced it to the brink of collapse. It was acquired by another banking giant, ČSOB, for one Czech crown.

Despite its strategic location along the Old Town's ramparts, the Powder Tower (Prašná Brána) was designed with pomp—rather than military might—in mind. Replacing a two-hundred-year-old gate so dilapidated that locals nicknamed it "Threadbare," the new tower was designed to lend gravitas to the adjacent Royal Court residence and serve as a ceremonial gateway to the Royal Route, where Bohemian kings staged lavish processions. Construction began under architect Matěj Rejsek in 1475, but halted after eight years when riots impelled King Vladislav II to relocate the Royal Court to Prague Castle. The unfinished tower was given a makeshift roof and was used to store gunpowder, thus its name. Unfortunately, its ad hoc role made it an obvious target for enemies. It was badly damaged in 1757 by Prussian troops, and much of its battered ornamentation was removed shortly thereafter. The tower stood neglected until 1823, when a clock was installed in its facade, giving it a new lease on life.

A unique remnant of medieval Prague, the Powder Tower still sternly demarcates the border between the city's Old and New towns. It now stands rather incongruously at the eastern end of Na Příkopě, the bustling commercial boulevard that runs along the Old Town's former fortification wall, and in stark contrast to the adjoining Municipal House—a grand Art Nouveau confection built in 1911 on the former site of the Royal Court. The tower's heightened silhouette is the work of architect Josef Mocker, who renovated the tower in the late nineteenth century, removing the clock and adding the work of leading sculptors of the day to the facade. He also gave the tower a distinct silhouette, with a steeply pitched roof and spiked turrets. The Powder Tower is a popular gathering point for tourists, who can climb the stairs to the top for an aerial view of Celetná Street—once the path of royal processions, now a busy pedestrian route.

In 1383, King Wenceslas IV abandoned the castle and moved the Royal Court. The new site was on the border of the New Town, which Wenceslas's father, Charles IV, had founded thirty-five years earlier. It was a thriving crossroads of distant trade routes and provided a stark contrast to the sequestered castle atmosphere. It served as the residence of Bohemian rulers for a century, before religious riots in the area led King Vladislav II to move back to the castle. The abandoned residence was left to deteriorate, until cardinal Arnošt Harrach established an archbishop's seminary there in 1631. After a fire in 1689, the complex was rebuilt. In 1776, after the seminary relocated to the Clementinum, the army moved in, converting the complex into a military barracks and later into an academy. In 1902, the complex was demolished as part of the citywide redevelopment.

Built on the site of the Royal Court in 1911, the Art Nouveau Municipal House (Obecní Dům) is the most extravagant product of the boom times that swept through Prague with the industrial revolution. Exemplifying the artistic and structural possibilities spawned by such newfound materials as iron and glass, the curvaceous domed structure with a rhomboid footprint was designed by architects Antonín Balšánek and Osvald Polívka. The wealth of masterful mosaics, murals, and sculptures embellishing every square inch was the

collaborative effort of prominent Czech artists, including Alphonse Mucha, Karel Špillar, and Ladislav Šaloun. An exuberant symbol of the democratic spirit of the times, the Municipal House was chosen as the site where the Czechoslovak state was signed into independence in 1918. Today it hosts lavish balls, art exhibitions, and musical events, including the Prague Spring Festival. Musical performances are held in the building's renowned Smetana Concert Hall, now home of the Prague Symphony Orchestra.

In the Middle Ages, the Romanesque Church of St. Benedict was erected just inside the Old Town's borders in the vicinity of the Royal Court. During Hussite times, the church grew obsolete, and in 1676 the Premonstratension College of St. Norbert was erected on the site. In 1793, at the behest of Empress Maria Theresa, the college became home to the Institute for Noble Women—a charitable home for impoverished women of irreproachable morals and aristocratic lineage. The institute later moved up to a more prestigious site at Prague Castle, and the entire college complex was demolished in 1928, revealing an odd panorama of staid apartment buildings juxtaposed with the Baroque tower of the thirteenth-century Church of St. James located on Malá Štupartská Street. In the 1930s, a row of one-story modern structures, housing airline ticketing offices and other commercial ventures, filled the gap, which was bordered on its northern side by the Kotva Insurance Company's interwar high-rise.

The mother of all Communist-era department stores, Kotva (the Anchor) opened its doors in 1975. Designed by Věra and Vladimír Machonin, the building was based on a honeycomb structure that comprised a massive cluster of hexagonal sections of reinforced cast concrete, supported on pillars and glazed with brown glass. In its early years, Kotva attracted tens of thousands of customers a day, many who traveled from the far reaches of the Eastern Bloc. Kotva no longer monopolizes the retail sector the way it once did, but it remains one of Prague's busier stores, providing Western brand names in fashion, cosmetics, and electronics. In 2005, construction began on a potential threat just across Revoluční Street—the massive Palladium shopping mall, slated for opening in 2007. Kotva's current owner, the Irish company Markland Holdings, insists that the two complexes will be complementary and the possibility of building a connecting pedestrian bridge has even been raised.

With the establishment of the New Town in 1348, an expansive swath of land surrounding the Old Town walls was designated for redevelopment. Among those negatively affected by Charles IV's ambitious urban plan were the inhabitants of a thriving Romanesque palace settlement, located opposite the former Royal Court overlooking Náměstí Republiky (Republic Square). They were resettled, their homes were razed, and the cleared site was built upon several times. In the mid-1600s, the Church of St. Joseph and a Capuchin monastery were erected on the site. The military, which already occupied the Royal Court building across the street, took over the monastery in 1795 and converted it into a barracks. By the mid-1800s the army had outgrown the building, so the neo-Romanesque Joseph Barracks, shown here, were erected to accommodate their needs. By then, Republic Square had evolved into a busy transport hub, crisscrossed with tramlines connecting the medieval Old Town with its burgeoning new counterpart.

As of 2006, the largest shopping mall in Prague was being developed on the 3.5-acre site occupied by the former Joseph Barracks. The $325-million project, dubbed the Palladium, will comprise over forty thousand square feet of shops and restaurants, as well as offices and a massive underground parking lot. The construction site, however, was temporarily transformed into a large-scale archaeological dig as remarkable findings were discovered during site preparations. Previously undocumented remains, including a twelfth-century Romanesque palace, two stone houses, and a dozen wooden structures, as well as three thousand boxes of pottery, fine glass, and coins, were unearthed, proving that the medieval suburbs of the Old Town were far more extensive and luxurious than previously believed. Historians are faced with rewriting several chapters of the city's early history. Meanwhile, the developers plan to integrate some of the findings into their retail complex, perhaps under a glass walkway, enabling shoppers to peruse the Romanesque ruins in situ.

In 1355, Charles IV was crowned leader of the Holy Roman Empire in Italy. Upon returning to Prague, he founded the St. Ambrosius Church and monastery, in commemoration of his coronation in a church of the same name in Milan. Located just outside of the historic city walls, the project was part of Charles's ongoing push to develop the New Town. Milanese Benedictines initially ran St. Ambrosius, until Irish Franciscan monks—having fallen out of favor with Elizabeth I—took over in 1630. U Hybernů comes from *Hibernia*, the Latin word for Ireland. The friars renovated the buildings, commissioning Carlo Lurago to build the Baroque Church of Immaculate Conception of the Virgin Mary and planting "exotic" potato plants in the garden. In 1786, the building was closed and deconsecrated, and was later given a neoclassical facelift and converted into a customhouse. This photo is from 1932, before it underwent yet another transformation, this time into one of Prague's largest and most popular exhibition halls.

Providing an elegant visual counterweight to the Powder Tower across the street, U Hybernů's monumental facade is one of Prague's most significant examples of neoclassical architecture. The complex's latest transformation entails its conversion into a world-class musical theater, designed to rival the Municipal House located across the street. The project has, however, sparked opposition, as certain historically significant sections of the church—including both pillars of the triumphal arch—have been removed to make way for the stage. The building has been a source of controversy for over a decade now; in 1993, then–minister of culture Jindřich Kabát allegedly used the property, along with the House at the Black Madonna, as collateral for a loan from a Czech bank in order to start a state-run lottery to finance cultural projects. The lottery went bankrupt after four months, Kabát was acquitted, and the city covered his debt to prevent the historical monument from being confiscated.

With increasing numbers of tourists and business travelers coming to Prague in the mid-1800s, hotels began sprouting up just outside the Old Town's borders. Situated opposite the Powder Tower, on the corner of Na Příkopě and Hybernska streets, the Blue Star Hotel was erected in 1846 and became one of the city's more popular hotels. Shown here in 1934, it was later immortalized in the 1941 Czech film *The Blue Star Hotel*. To its right stood the headquarters of one of the city's leading financial institutions, Živnostenská banka. Crowned with sculptor Antonín Popp's statue *Genius with the Lion*, the neo-Renaissance building with Art Nouveau elements was constructed in 1900 by architect Osvald Polívka who, shortly thereafter, would commence work on the Municipal House across the street. The completion of the latter in 1912 proved a boon for the nearby hotels, as visiting musicians and composers provided a lucrative customer base, including Hector Berlioz and Frédéric Chopin, who both stayed at the Blue Star during their visits to Prague.

By the late 1920s, Prague had grown into a bastion of domestic capital for Bohemia, as well as a strategic base for Western European funds heading east. Having outgrown its headquarters, Živnostenská banka purchased the Blue Star and Black Horse hotels to either side, subsequently razing them along with the Polívka's original bank building. Topped with Popp's statue, which was transplanted from the old bank building, the monumental, granite-clad structure was created in a Modernist-Classicist style by František Roith and completed in 1942. It fully accommodated the bank's expanding operations and stood as a symbol of the institution's prominent role on the financial stage. It was the country's most powerful bank when it was taken over and merged into the Communist banking system in the 1950s. Today the headquarters of Česká národní banka (Czech National Bank), it is one of many bank buildings on Na Příkopě, which is now known as "Prague's Wall Street."

Na Příkopě Street became home to a plethora of bank buildings and financial institutions erected during the economic boom of the early twentieth century. The headquarters of the Czech Bank Union stood in the middle of the street until 1926, when the bank decided to expand. Their building was demolished, along with five adjacent structures extending through the block, creating a massive lot linking Na Příkopě with the medieval fruit market. Their plans, however, were abandoned, and in the 1930s the lot was occupied by the Myslbek Arts Association pavilion (named after sculptor Josef Václav Myslbek), as well as some modest commercial structures facing Na Příkopě, shown here in 1945. After the pavilion was dismantled in the 1950s, the entire area was converted into an expansive urban park. In the 1970s, during renovation work on the Metro, and later the nearby Estates Theater, the site became a makeshift construction site.

One of Prague's first large-scale commercial developments after the fall of communism, the Myslbek Shopping and Office Complex was the most heavily scrutinized and hotly debated project of the early 1990s. Completed in 1996, the multipurpose structure was designed by local architects Zdeněk Hölzel and Jan Kerel, in collaboration with the renowned French architect Claude Parent. While respecting the height of the neighboring historical buildings, the design is unusual, with a multilayered glass-and-steel facade on the Na Příkopě side, and distinctive diagonal elements representing the creation of a new order. The mobile gate superimposed over the facade recalls the gates that punctuated the Old Town's fortification wall, which ran along Na Příkopě in medieval times. The building incorporates a distinct Prague phenomenon, the *pasáž*, or pedestrian passage, which here serves as a shopping arcade extending the length of the ground floor and linking the Old Town's medieval fruit market area with the New Town's bustling commercial district.

Kilián Ignác Dientzenhofer (1689–1751) was undeniably one of Prague's greatest proponents of the Baroque style, designing some of the city's most impressive and lavish monuments, including St. Nicholas's Church and the Goltz-Kinský Palace in Old Town Square. One of his lesser known—but no less impressive—secular constructions is the stunning Baroque-Rococo Piccolomini Palace on Na Příkopě, shown here in 1909. It was built between 1743 and 1751 for Prince Ottavio Piccolomini, whose family had settled in Bohemia after the Battle of White Mountain. Like many of Dientzenhofer's works, it was realized in collaboration with his pupil and son-in-law Anselmo Lurago. Its richly decorated symmetrical facade features the sculptures of Ignác Platzer, who also created statues for St. Nicholas's Church in the Lesser Quarter (Malá Strana), on which Dientzenhofer was working simultaneously. The elegant building came to be known as Palais Savarin and housed the popular Savarin café.

Located at the bustling intersection of Na Příkopě and Havířská Street, the building, now known as the Sylva-Taroucca Palace, houses a bizarre array of commercial enterprises. Its upper floor contains the Casino Palais Savarin, replete with high-tech slot machines, blackjack tables, and shiny roulette wheels. Next door is the Museum of Communism, where some of the harsh realities of Soviet-era Prague are on display, including a grim interrogation room and a grocery store with bare shelves. On the ground floor is the ultimate symbol of the global economy, McDonald's, whose red umbrellas and aluminum chairs spill out onto the street. Also on the ground floor is a currency exchange, a Black Light Theater ticket outlet, and an updated version of the Savarin café. Though its original Baroque splendor is looking a bit worse for the wear, the palace has evolved into a thriving commercial building, located in the heart of one of the city's main shopping districts.

Na Příkopě, which means "on the moat," developed along the Old Town's fortification wall, where a moat once existed. When the New Town was established in 1348, plans to fill in the moat fell by the wayside, causing a host of problems for the increasingly populated area. Residents made a nasty habit of tipping chamber pots into the moat. Equally haphazard was the narrow road built above the moat; more than a few horse carriages tumbled off it into the foul water below. In 1760 the moat was finally filled in, creating a wide boulevard ripe for development. The site at the corner of Na Příkopě and Wenceslas Square (Václavské Náměstí) was one of the first to be utilized. By 1860, it was home to the U Špinků building, shown on the right in this 1890 photo. The popular Café Viennese (Kavárna Vídeňská) on the first floor was patronized by the intelligentsia of the day, including František Palacký and J. L. Rieger.

Apart from being its "Wall Street," Na Příkopě is also Prague's "Fifth Avenue," one of the city's swankier thoroughfares, where Czech and international retailers operate out of the street's many historical buildings. Koruna Palace, shown on the right, sits on the site of the former U Špinků. Designed in 1912 by Antonín Pfeiffer and Matěj Blecha, the Palace was one of Prague's first reinforced concrete structures and is a fusion of streamlined Art Deco and stylized Art Nouveau elements. The building included offices and apartments in the upper floors, a glass-ceilinged café on the ground floor, and a swimming pool in the basement. In the 1970s, a ground-floor passage was built to access the newly built Můstek underground station. The Palace's current state is the result of major renovations in the 1990s. The modern shopping center houses a diverse array of luxury stores, fast-food outlets, and the Bontonland music megastore, which occupies a three-story area created over the former swimming pool.

In the 1840s, the idea of building a national theater, by and for the Czech people, became a patriotic obsession that would last three decades. A fund-raising campaign dubbed "People for Themselves" was launched in 1851, eventually raising enough money to purchase the site of a former salt works, located on the corner of the Vltava embankment and Národní Avenue. On May 16, 1868, twenty thousand Czechs proudly witnessed the laying of the foundation stone, while the Hapsburg rulers bristled. Designed by Josef Zítek, the building was a unique blend of neo-Renaissance architecture and Slavonic symbolism, representing the coalescence of a new Czech aesthetic and identity. Just as the finishing touches were being made in August 1881, a catastrophic fire broke out, destroying much of the building. Undeterred, organizers held a new fund-raiser; the theater was rebuilt, and in November 1883, it was inaugurated with a performance of *Libuše*, an opera about the mythical birth of the Czech nation, composed for the occasion by Bedřich Smetana.

Standing proudly on the Vltava, topped with statues of Lady Victory riding horse-drawn chariots into the future, the gold-encrusted National Theater represents the acme of the Czech cultural renaissance. The artists who contributed to its realization are now known as the National Theater Generation. One of Prague's main cultural venues, the theater now hosts year-round performances of opera, drama, and dance. In 1977, it closed down for six years of major renovation. The original building was spruced up and kept intact, while reconstructions occurred backstage to meet the logistical demands of contemporary performances. The theater's antiquated electrical system was rewired, the actors' facilities were modernized, and a large tunnel was built, connecting the historical building with a new underground depository for stage sets and large equipment. In 1983, more than a century after its inauguration, the updated theater was reopened to the public with a nostalgic performance of Smetana's *Libuše*.

At the end of the nineteenth century, the character of Národní Avenue would be drastically altered by several key events, including the erection of the National Theater at the avenue's westernmost end, along with the construction of the adjacent riverside embankment and the new Legions Bridge across the river. Národní Avenue grew in importance and grandeur and became a favored route for ceremonial processions heading toward Wenceslas Square. Its character would undergo another major transformation in the 1930s, as the thriving National Theater had by then outgrown its site and plans were made for expansion. The site of the adjoining Choura Houses, pictured here in 1935, seemed an obvious choice. The buildings that housed residential and office spaces, as well as ground-floor retail stores—including a popular hair salon and party-supply store—were demolished in the late 1950s to make way for the theater's new annex.

The hulking glass-and-steel mass of the Nová Scéna (New Scene) theater, erected in 1983 on the site of the razed Choura Houses, counts among the monumental architectural oddities built in Prague under communism. Leading functionalist architect Bohuslav Fuchs won the competition for the project in the 1960s, but he died before work began, and the project was eventually handed to Karel Prager of Prague's Institute of Construction. Surfaced in over four thousand glass panels and featuring an inward-slanting roofline, the structure was supposed to reflect—both literally and structurally—the form of the adjacent National Theater. The modern interiors designed by Prager in collaboration with a group of Czech artists are a striking combination of sweeping contours, rendered in emerald serpentine marble and dark woods, with sculptural lighting fixtures and modern leather and steel furnishings. The theater and its high-tech circular stage are home to Laterna Magika, one of Prague's most innovative multimedia performance groups.

With the rise of the Hapsburgs following the Thirty Years' War in the mid-1600s, Prague developed into a Baroque expression of Catholic domination. A single-nave Baroque church was erected on Resslova Street between 1730 and 1740 under the guidance of architects Pavel Ignác Bayer, Kilián Ignac Dientzenhofer, and Kristián Spannbrucker. It served as a home for retired Catholic priests and—very conveniently—there was an extensive crypt with 112 alcoves for priests' tombs located underground. In 1783, Emperor Joseph II converted the church into a military barracks, and in 1869 it became a center for Czech technology, with a model of a sugar-refinery displayed in the nave. As an urban standardization measure in 1885, the surrounding pavement was lowered several feet, giving the church a raised appearance, as seen here in 1890. In 1933, the building was leased to the Czechoslovak Orthodox Church, which renovated the church and dedicated it to saints Cyril and Methodius, ninth-century apostles to the Slavs.

During the Nazi occupation, the church's crypt served as the final refuge of Jozef Gabčík and Jan Kubiš, the British-trained Czechoslovak sergeants who parachuted into Prague and assassinated Reinhard Heydrich, Nazi commander and prime mover of the "final solution," who died on June 4, 1942. In malicious retaliation, the Nazis razed the nearby villages of Lidice and Ležáky, arresting thousands and executing all male residents over the age of sixteen. A fevered hunt for the assassins was launched, and on June 18, 1942, German soldiers assaulted the church, bombarding it with gunfire and flooding the crypt. Gabčík, Kubiš, and five other parachutists held out for several hours before three of them fell and the situation's futility led those remaining to take their own lives. The church now houses the National Memorial to the Heroes of the Heydrich Terror exhibition, commemorating what Václav Havel called "one of the most significant acts of resistance on a pan-European scale." Havel added, "We finished the war as a victorious state and not as a defeated one." A plaque (above) dedicated to the "Heroes of the Heydrich Terror" is mounted on the crypt's outer wall, which remains riddled with Nazi bullet holes.

Starting in the mid-1800s, a series of embankments was constructed along the right side of the Vltava, extending along the borders of the Old Town to Vyšehrad in the south. The embankments spurred development along the riverside, which the city had turned its back on for far too long. Built downriver from the National Theater at the start of the twentieth century, the Rašín Embankment became home to an elegant stretch of Art Nouveau and neo-Renaissance apartment buildings, including Václav Havel's childhood home in an apartment building—seen above with a small domed roof—erected by his grandfather, real-estate mogul Václav M. Havel. On the corner, adjacent to the Havel property, stood a neo-Renaissance building which met its untimely fate on February 14, 1945, when sixty Flying Fortresses from the U.S. 8th Air Force mistook Prague for Dresden. The aircraft—sixty-five miles off course—dropped 152 tons of bombs on the city. The experience no doubt left the nine-year-old Havel to contemplate the follies of war.

Following the Velvet Revolution in 1989, newly elected president Václav Havel spearheaded plans to develop the empty lot he had grown up next to. The result was one of Prague's most iconoclastic and controversial buildings. Completed in 1995, the Dancing House (Tančící Dům) was bankrolled by Dutch company Nationale Nederlanden, and designed by Havel's friend and neighbor, architect Vlado Milunič. The world-renowned Frank Gehry also joined the project after another high-profile architect, Jean Nouvel, declined due to the site's small size (5,000 square feet). The Deconstructivist design is intended to symbolize Czechoslovak society in transition—the straighter tower representing the static totalitarian past and the "crushed can" glass tower symbolizing the dynamic future. Such symbolism, however, is often obscured by the pop-culture reference to "Fred and Ginger," which the building has been affectionately nicknamed because its silhouette recalls the Hollywood dancers.

In an attempt to keep Slavic traditions alive, Charles IV founded Na Slovanech (meaning "at the Slavs") church and monastery in 1347. The Gothic complex was built on a prominent terraced site overlooking the Vltava in the Vyšehrad district. Charles extended his welcome to monks from all Slav countries to settle at the complex and make it their regional headquarters. Over the centuries, the complex changed hands several times, with each occupant leaving their distinctive brand of religious symbolism on the architecture. In the mid-fifteenth century, the Hussites founded a monastery here. In the seventeenth century, Spanish Benedictines moved in, rebuilding the church in the Baroque style and adding two towers to the facade. In 1880, neo-Gothic alterations were undertaken by German Benedictines from Beuron. However, the most radical change came in 1945, when the infamous air raid ravaged the towers and caused the collapse of the church vaulting.

Extensive renovations commenced a year after the bombing; the first decade was spent reinforcing the church's infrastructure and stabilizing bay upon bay of massive vaulting and trusses. The monastery's interior was remodeled to house the Czechoslovak Academy of Sciences, and what remained of the monastery's phenomenal wall frescoes was painstakingly preserved. In the 1950s, plans to restore the facade in the image of its former self lost momentum in favor of less traditional options. A competition was held, and František Černý's iconoclastic proposal—comprising a pair of overlapping parabolic spires—won out. Today, the spired church stands as one of the most striking silhouettes on Prague's skyline. Though steadfastly modern, its design harkens back to the original Gothic high gable and the seventeenth-century Baroque towers while also providing a visual transition between the old church buildings and the more modern structures erected in the vicinity.

The movement of timber on the Vltava had been a thriving industry since medieval times. Logs, strapped together to form rafts, were typically floated in from the forested hinterlands of southern Bohemia and docked in the Podskalí district, located just beneath the Vyšehrad bluff. Here, the wood was inventoried, processed, and then sold for construction, firewood, and other purposes. One of the area's main buildings was the Na Výtoni customhouse, where duties were collected on the timber. The word *výtoň* comes from the Czech verb *vytínati*—"to cut off." When the rafts arrived at the Výton checkpoint, a certain length of timber was cut off and collected as a tax. The original timber building dates back to the 1500s and was modified several times. Bearing the New Town emblem over its portal, it was converted in the mid-nineteenth century into the U Koppů restaurant and pub—pictured here in 1908—which was a popular haunt among the rafters of Prague until the disappearance of the Podskalí district.

At the turn of the century, reforms—including the construction of the Rašín Embankment, the Vyšehrad Railway Bridge, and the Vyšehrad Tunnel—would severely change Podskalí. Today, the Na Výtoni customhouse stands as a lone remnant of the areas's once-flourishing river industry. As a flood protection measure, much of the district's street level was elevated. Na Výtoni, which originally stood on land gently sloping down to the river, now sits in a sunken plot surrounded by streets heavily trafficked by trams and vehicles. The house was purchased by the city in 1908 in order to preserve it as a historical monument. The ground floor still houses a popular Czech pub, while its upper floor contains an exhibition curated by the Museum of the City of Prague, dedicated to the bygone Podskalí workers—the rafters, boaters, lumberers, sand-miners, and fishermen—whose lives were inextricably linked to the Vltava.

The flood of 1890, which engulfed much of Podskalí, prompted the massive redevelopment of the area, including regulating the Vltava, constructing the Rašín Embankment, and demolishing numerous buildings. Quaint historical houses, fishermen's shelters, and lumberyards were among the structures that fell prey to the citywide reforms. Located just downriver from Na Výtoni, in the shadow of the Vyšehrad promontory topped with the Church of St. Peter and Paul, the modest Libusinka Brewery was among several riverside businesses that provided local workers with a bit of respite. By 1907, however, the pub was on the verge of demolition and stood in a state of disrepair, all of its windows boarded up, yet the Czech sign above the doorway still asked passersby to "Try Beer From Braník," recalling better days. The character of Podskalí would be irrrevocably altered as city planners—along with ambitious real estate agents and speculators—made plans to transform the area into a new residential quarter.

The redevelopment of Podskalí coincided with the birth of Czech Cubist architecture. As a result, a remarkable cluster of Cubist buildings were constructed in the area in the early 1900s. With its prismatic shapes and oblique angles, the Villa Kovařovič, shown here, is a brilliant example of how Czech architects translated the ideas of Picasso and Braque into architectural forms, with dramatic plays of light and shadow. Its designer, pioneering architect Josef Chochol, also built a condominium complex and the Hodek apartment building in close proximity, while his architectural peers, Otakar Novotný and Emil Králíček, constructed their own versions of Cubist-style villas on either side of Villa Kovárovič. Despite the elitist theories surrounding Cubism—including the dynamism of the human spirit and the fracturing of atomic matter—these villas were built for ordinary folk, including proprietors of construction companies, many of whom erected these unprecedented structures for themselves.

Vyšehrad, the rocky headland on the Vltava's right bank, is the mythological wellspring of Prague. According to legend, it was from here that the Slavic medieval princess Libuše ruled over Bohemia. When pressed by gender-biased members of her tribe to find a male counterpart to rule, she married Přemysl, a young plowman, who gave his name to Bohemia's founding dynasty. In the tenth century, the Přemyslid rulers began constructing a castle atop Vyšehrad. First occupied by Vratislav II around 1070, the castle at Vyšehrad would serve as their seat of power for seventy years, before it was abandoned in favor of the Přemyslids' former royal residence located atop Hradčany hill across the river. The Vyšehrad plateau juts out in the west, forming a sheer rock wall dropping into the river. Originally a vital defensive position, it would later prove a major transportation obstacle, cutting off traffic running along the southern shores. Prior to the construction of the Vyšehrad tunnel, ferry operators—shown here in 1890 in front of the Vyšehrad ferry house—provided the primary means of circumventing the rocky outcrop.

The redevelopment of the Podskalí district following the devastating flood of 1890 entailed boring a tunnel through Vyšehrad rock in 1902. At the same time, the Rašín and Podolské embankments were constructed to its north and south, respectively. The collective result was a major transportation route for vehicular and tram traffic, running down the Vltava's right bank and connecting the city of Prague to southern Bohemia. With its cylindrical towers and battlements, the entrance to the hundred-foot-long tunnel was designed in a romantic style, echoing the medieval castle ruins above. The gable-roof building on the hill now houses the Vyšehrad Art Gallery. Poised below, on the outer ridge, are the remains of the Gothic guard tower that, according to legend, originally served as the "Baths of Libuše," where the mighty princess bathed with her lovers before hurling them over the rock. To the left of the tunnel entrance stands the Baroque-style watchman's house, where tunnel tolls were once collected.

The origins of the Church of Saints Peter and Paul date back to the eleventh century, when Vratislav II moved the royal residence across the river, from the castle at Hradčany to the fortified settlement at Vyšehrad. Determined to create a castle worthy of his kingdom and rivaling Hradčany in scale and form, Vratislav initiated a major building program that included fortifications, a palace, and the Church of Saints Peter and Paul. So dedicated to the church was the king that he reportedly carried baskets of stones and sand to the site on his shoulders. Originally a Romanesque three-nave basilica, the church was altered over the centuries according to the styles of the time. Under King Charles IV in the mid-fourteenth century, it was transformed into a Gothic five-nave structure with lateral chapels. Renaissance alterations were made in the sixteenth century, followed by an extensive refurbishment in the 1720s, which included the addition of the elegant, curvaceous facade shown here in 1901.

The church underwent a radical transformation in 1902 when it was given an exaggerated neo-Gothic facade with two towering spires that now dominate Vyšehrad's skyline. Designed by architect František Mikš, it is sometimes attributed to Josef Mocker, who was known for giving buildings neo-Gothic face-lifts. Mocker's late nineteenth-century work, however, was confined to the interior layout, which he completely revamped in the neo-Gothic style, stripping the interior of many of its Renaissance and Baroque elements while choosing somewhat uncharacteristically to leave the Baroque facade intact. The church's most recent renovation in 2002 led to the discovery of what is believed to be a relic of St. Valentine—supposedly part of Charles IV's extensive relic collection—housed in one of the church's depository shrines. The church is a functioning house of worship, with regular services that include a special annual mass for lovers on St. Valentine's Day.

After seeing the *pièce de résistance* of the Paris World Exhibition in 1889—the Eiffel Tower—the Czechs decided they wanted one for themselves. Erected atop Petřín Hill overlooking Malá Strana, Bohemia's version of the Eiffel Tower debuted two years later as part of the 1891 Jubilee Exhibition. Erected in just five months under the guidance of engineer František Prášil, the 200-foot tower epitomized the newfound wonders of turn-of-the-century iron engineering and heralded the country's growing sophistication, which, by association, would be on a par with Parisian culture. A funicular railway, built specifically to transport visitors to the tower, ran on a water overbalance system on rails extending from Újezd Street in Malá Strana to the top of Petřín Hill. The tower was about a fifth of the size of the original in Paris, though measured from sea level, the two towers were approximately equal in height.

The Petřín Tower remains a bit of an oddity amid Prague's renowned "one hundred spires." During the Nazi occupation, Hitler apparently considered it an eyesore and wanted it dismantled, but somehow it survived. In the 1950s, the tower was fitted with transmitting equipment and was used to broadcast TV signals across town, a role it maintained into the 1990s, when more high-tech towers rendered it obsolete. The transmitter closed down in 1992 and a major renovation in 2000 removed the broadcasting equipment and revived the tower's defunct lift. Now, visitors wanting to see a bird's-eye view of Prague from the tower's observatory have the option of treading up 299 steps or being whisked to the top by an elevator. Nearby is the Mirror Maze, located in a mini faux-castle that was also built for the 1891 exhibition.

From high atop Petřín Hill, the stunning panorama of Prague in 1863 shows the Old Town to the left and the New Town to the right, with the beautiful Francis I Bridge spanning the Vltava in the foreground. A major engineering feat for its day, the chain bridge was completed in 1841 and was the first structure to cross the Vltava since Charles Bridge was erected upstream nearly 500 years before. Midway, it crosses over Shooter's Island, where marksmen once practiced their skills. The bridge extends across the river onto Národní Avenue, which runs along the Old Town's former fortification wall, and along with Prague's other first great boulevards—Wenceslas Square and Na Příkopě Avenue—forms what is known as the Golden Cross. The construction of the chain bridge and the adjacent embankment fueled development along the riverside, including the French Renaissance luxury apartment block built on the northern side of Národní Avenue in 1862 by Ignác Ullmann.

Today, the same panorama offers a visual timeline of Prague's evolution—extending from the city's historical core around the Vltava, through the suburbs of Vinohrady and Žižkov, and onward toward the horizon, punctuated with the futuristic Žižkov TV Tower. The monumental gold-crested National Theater, erected in the late 1800s, now stands on the right side of Národní Avenue, on the site of a former salt house. Across the street, on the first floor of Ullmann's building, is the famed Slavia Café, where Czech writers and dissidents—including Václav Havel in his prepresidential days—would come to discuss their latest works and the overthrow of communism. The Francis I Bridge was replaced in 1901 with the granite Legions Bridge, which has a wide staircase leading down onto Shooter's Island. The marksmen are long gone and the lush island now hosts outdoor film screenings and an annual puppet festival in the summer months.

When Charles IV founded the New Town in 1348, he designated a stretch of land outside the town's eastern border for cultivating grapes in order to keep the royal wine cellars properly stocked. The verdant area, called Královské Vinohrady (Royal Vineyards), later became a popular place for leisure activities and building summer houses. In the 1870s, when the city ramparts were dismantled, the area underwent a construction boom, and by the turn of the twentieth century it was a wealthy suburb with grand Art Nouveau, neo-Renaissance, and neo-Baroque buildings lining its streets. Situated at Vinohrady's eastern border, Jiří z Poděbrad Square (named after the Bohemian Hussite king Jiří of Poděbrady) was an urban expanse used for recreational purposes, seasonal festivities, and markets. The street on the right in this photograph, Vinohradská (known as Stalinova Street during Communist rule), is the area's main artery, feeding into the city center via the upper end of Wenceslas Square.

The massive Church of the Sacred Heart now dominates Jiří z Poděbrad Square. Built between 1929 an 1932, the structure was designed by Slovenian architect Josip Plečnik, best known for his masterful renovations to Prague Castle in the 1920s. Plečnik apparently gleaned inspiration from myriad sources, including the Parthenon, the story of Noah's ark, and Cubism, among others. The result is a structure nonpareil in Prague, anticipating the stylistic promiscuity of postmodernism half a century later. The base of the single-nave church is clad in dark brown brick decorated with light gray tabs that jut out at regular intervals. Out of this heavy base rises a white neoclassical structure. Flanked by obelisks, the slablike tower at the rear is punctured with a glass-faced clock. The church is a functioning house of worship with services held daily. In the background is the futuristic Žižkov Television Tower, completed in 1992 and now adorned with David Černý's crawling baby sculptures.

Poised atop Vítkov Hill, the brilliant one-eyed Hussite general Jan Žižka watches over the city in the form of what is reputedly the world's largest equestrian statue, weighing in at 16.5 tons. In 1420, Žižka led a decisive battle atop Vitkov Hill, trouncing Emperor Sigismund and his papal forces, thereby ensuring Hussite dominance. Žižka's statue stands atop the even-more-massive National Memorial. Designed by Jan Zázvorka, the austere granite structure was erected in 1932 in commemoration of the Legionnaires who fought the Austro-Hungarian empire in World War I. The once-beloved memorial, however, became estranged to many Czechs under communism, when it was converted into a memorial dedicated to party leaders. Shown here in 1962 is an approved Communist version of the original Czech coat of arms, which was stripped of the symbols of the cross and crown and embellished with a star over the lion's head.

These days, the National Memorial that has solemnly served the political aims of nationalists, fascists, and Communists throughout the years is undergoing an identity crisis. Occasional political ceremonies are still held there, though the site is better known among the younger set for hosting dance raves and an annual multimedia exhibition featuring audio-video installations and avant garde dance performances, dramatically staged within the building's cavernous interior. The site also doubled as the "Bureau for Paranormal Research and Defense" in the film *Hellboy*, shot in Prague in 2003. Not surprisingly, the monument's commercial transformation began after the fall of communism in 1989, when the Czech coat of arms was remounted and the Ministry of Culture leased the monument to entrepreneur Vratislav Čekan, who had plans of redeveloping Vitkov Hill and the adjacent Žižkov area. In the meantime, Čekan rented the memorial out for lavish galas, where Prague's well-heeled set sipped cocktails amid sarcophagi.

While Prague has long been renowned as the "city of a hundred spires," its suburb of Smíchov, located on the Vltava's left bank, gained the dubious title of "hundred-chimney Manchester." Up until the late nineteenth century, Smíchov was a decidedly lush area, characterized by gardens, vineyards, hop fields, and aristocratic summer houses. The industrial revolution brought about a radical transformation of the area, with numerous factories establishing themselves there, including mass producers of chemicals, china, and chocolate, as well as the Staropramen Brewery, the Ringhoffer railway carriage factory, and the Walter aircraft engine company. In conjunction with the factories, a working-class neighborhood developed, with residential houses, workers' camps, and small businesses such as the Golden Angel Inn—shown here in the early 1900s—located at the tram crossing at Plzeňská and Nádražní streets. As factories began to modernize and move further afield in the mid-1900s, Smíchov started its general decline.

The dramatic undulating form of the Zlatý Anděl (Golden Angel) building, designed by French architect Jean Nouvel in 2000, now sits on the site of the former Golden Angel Inn. Developed by the Dutch company ING, the massive complex includes offices and retail spaces built over the busy Anděl metro station. On the tower's facade, Nouvel incorporated the image of a guardian angel—namely Bruno Ganz, the actor-angel from Wim Wenders's 1987 film *Wings of Desire*. The wraparound glass facade also features images of clouds drifting across the transparent wall and fragments of poetry on the subject of angels by Franz Kafka, Gustav Meyrink, Rainer Maria Rilke, and other authors closely linked to Prague. Anchoring the neighborhood, the massive complex has spurred development and helped to transform the neglected industrial area into a crowded commercial district—a brilliant manifestation of Nouvel's theory of "urban acupuncture," whereby strategic insertions serve to release latent urban energy.

The rapid industrialization of Prague in the nineteenth century fueled the construction of no less than five new bridges across the Vltava River between 1840 and 1878. One of the most stunning was the Franz Josef I Bridge, completed in 1868, a superstructure for its day that extended from Revoluční Street across the river to the base of Letná Hill. The bridge was built by engineers William Henry Le Feuvre and Rowland Mason Ordish, the eminent London-based engineering team that went on to design the

Albert Bridge across the River Thames five years later, again using the chain suspension system Ordish had patented in 1858. Though the bridge, pictured here in 1900, later came to be called Štefánik Bridge, it was originally named after Emperor Franz Josef I, who spearheaded a range of large transportation projects during his reign, including an extensive railway system—also bearing his name—that crisscrossed Prague and connected it to neighboring countries.

By the late 1940s, Prague was a burgeoning metropolis, with increasing numbers of cars and buses plying its roads. The old chain bridge, originally built to handle pedestrian and horse-drawn traffic, no longer served the purposes of the developing city. It was dismantled in 1947 and replaced with a temporary wooden bridge, which stood for one year before being replaced by a reinforced concrete bridge that was completed in 1951. Designed by Jan Fischer and realized by Vlastislav Hofman and Otakar Širc, the new bridge was comprised of three distinct arches set atop granite-clad concrete piers. Built during the Communist regime, the structure was named Šverma Bridge in tribute to Jan Šverma, a Czech Communist and anti-Fascist fighter who died fighting Nazis in Slovakia in 1944. After the Velvet Revolution, when many structures were stripped of their Communist names, the bridge retained its name, perhaps because Šverma—who died before he could witness the full blight of the Communists—escaped total vilification.

In the last decade of the nineteenth century, Prague was one of the industrial and cultural juggernauts of the Hapsburg empire. The 1891 Jubilee Exhibition was a means for Czechs to declare their modernity and propel themselves into the future. Laid out on the Holešovice corner of Stromovka Park by architects Antonín Wiehl and Bedřich Münzberger, the exposition included 146 buildings, an electricity network, a funicular tram, František Křižík's light fountain, and more—all designed to showcase the technological and engineering innovations of the day. Tributes to the Czech vernacular, such as Wiehl's Bohemian cottage, were particularly popular with fairgoers. The focal point was the massive glass-and-iron Industrial Palace, shown here. It was constructed by the First Bohemian Steelworks under the guidance of František Prášil, who also erected the Eiffel Tower replica on Petřín Hill. Over two million people visited the five-month exhibition, which was a source of pride and wonder for Czechs, and ultimately helped forge their emerging national identity.

Remarkably, the fairgrounds and major buildings have remained largely intact. The Industrial Palace now hosts exhibitions—ranging from auto shows, book fairs, and design expos to raunchier affairs such as the X-rated annual Erotica Sex Expo. Křižík's fountain remains the city's most spectacular ode to nineteenth-century ephemera, with spouting water jets and lasers now pulsing to the music of Dvořák, Smetana, Vangelis, Michael Jackson, and the *Hair* soundtrack, among others. Wiehl's pavilion, remodeled in the Baroque style, now houses the city's Lapidarium. In the late 1940s the park was used as a site for Communist congresses, and in the 1950s it was named after party hero Julius Fučík and became a Park of Culture and Relaxation. Soon after the Velvet Revolution, however, it was renamed simply Výstaviště (Exhibition Grounds) and renovated as part of the 1991 General Czechoslovak Exhibition, designed to commemorate a century of progress achieved, in spurts and fits, since the Jubilee Exhibition.

INDEX